RACIAL VIOLENCE AND HARASSMENT

The Policy Studies Institute (PSI) is Britain's leading independent research organisation undertaking studies of economic, industrial and social policy, and the workings of political institutions.

PSI is a registered charity, run on a non-profit basis, and is not associated with any political party, pressure group or commercial interest.

PSI attaches great importance to covering a wide range of subject areas with its multi-disciplinary approach. The Institute's researchers are organised in groups which currently cover the following programmes:

Crime, Justice and Youth Studies – Employment and Society – Ethnic Equality and Diversity – European Industrial Development – Fomily Finances – Information and Citizenship – Information and Cultural Studies – Social Care and Health Studies – Work, Benefits and Social Participation

This publication arises from the Ethnic Equality and Diversity group and is one of over 30 publications made available by the Institute each year.

Information about the work of PSI, and a catalogue of available books can be obtained from:

Marketing Department, PSI
100 Park Village East, London NW1 3SR

Racial Violence and Harassment

Satnam Virdee

1995

POLICY STUDIES INSTITUTE
London

The publishing imprint of the independent
POLICY STUDIES INSTITUTE
100 Park Village East, London NW1 3SR
Telephone: 0171-387 2171   Fax: 0171-388 0914

© Policy Studies Institute 1995

ISBN 0 85374 647 8

PSI Research Report 796

A CIP catalogue record of this book is available from the British Library.

1 2 3 4 5 6 7 8 9

PSI publications are available from
BEBC Distribution Ltd
P O Box 1496, Poole, Dorset, BH12 3YD

Books will normally be despatched within 24 hours. Cheques should be made payable to BEBC Distribution Ltd.

Credit card and telephone/fax orders may be placed on the following freephone numbers:

FREEPHONE: 0800 262260
FREEFAX: 0800 262266

Booktrade representation (UK & Eire):
Broadcast Books
24 De Montfort Road, London SW16 1LW
Telephone: 0181-677 5129

PSI subscriptions are available from PSI's subscription agent
Carfax Publishing Company Ltd
P O Box 25, Abingdon, Oxford OX14 3UE

Laserset by Policy Studies Institute
Printed in Great Britain by Redwood Books, Trowbridge, Wilts.

Contents

Acknowledgements

This report is the outcome of research funded by the Joseph Rowntree Charitable Trust. The study would not have been possible without the participation of the interviewees. I would like to thank them and the Race Relations Committee of the London Borough of Waltham Forest, the Afro-Caribbean Elders Association of Waltham Forest, Jobs Through English Training (JET), Purehart Services, Plus 4, and Anita Bedi for their support and help in finding the interviewees. Thanks are also due to Sharon Beishon, Raj Raithatha and Shamsa Rana for their assistance in carrying out the interviews.

I would also like to thank my colleagues at PSI for their help and support during the course of this study. In particular, I am grateful to Richard Berthoud, Pamela Meadows, Tariq Modood, Tim Newburn and David Smith (now of the University of Edinburgh) for their detailed comments on earlier drafts of the report. I would also like to thank all those outside PSI who by commenting on an earlier draft helped me to improve the book, particularly Dennis Brooks, Marion Fitzgerald and Paul Gordon.

1 Introduction

Objectives of the study

Racial violence and harassment is an issue of widespread public concern. It has been the subject of considerable coverage in the media recently with numerous television programmes and articles in the daily press devoted to describing and understanding the phenomenon. The problem and the measures required to address it effectively have also been the subject of debate within official circles (CRE 1994; Home Affairs Committee 1994; Parekh 1994).

Racial violence and harassment can take several forms, ranging from the relatively rare but serious incidents of murder and serious assaults to the more frequent incidents of racial abuse and threatening behaviour. Any discussion of how racial violence and harassment should be tackled needs to be based on a thorough understanding of the nature and scale of the problem. What sort of incident do members of minority ethnic groups themselves describe as 'racial harassment'? How seriously do they view different types of incident – individually or cumulatively? Whereabouts do these incidents occur, and who are the perpetrators? What, if anything, do the victims try to do about it? To what extent are people's lives affected beyond the actual racial violence and harassment that takes place?

The official figures on the extent of racial violence and harassment are based on police statistics and the British Crime Survey. These have been supplemented by a number of small-scale studies in local areas where racial violence and harassment is known to be a problem. This report reviews the evidence from these various sources, and adds a new one: detailed questioning about the experience of racial violence and harassment among a small sample of African Caribbean and South Asian families. The immediate objective is to understand the various levels and forms of harassment experienced by different minority ethnic groups in Britain.

Our eventual aim is to provide definitive measures of the extent of the problem, and an analysis of the types of incident experienced; to this end, questions have been asked of the sample of 5,000 African Caribbean and South Asian people in PSI's Fourth National Survey of Ethnic Minorities.

1

The results of that survey will be published in the winter of 1995/96. The purpose of this preliminary report is to describe and identify the various forms of racial harassment, to clarify the issues and to promote discussion and analysis of the problem.

Background to the problem

A number of key developments have contributed to bringing the problem of racial violence and harassment to the centre of public attention recently. The most important has been the concern surrounding several serious acts of racial violence such as that against Quaddus Ali described below.

> An Asian student was on a life-support machine after being beaten in what police have described as a racially-motivated incident... Quaddus Ali, aged 17 from Stepney in east London, was with three friends, all young men from the Bangladeshi community when he was set upon by eight young white people... Mr. Ali was punched and beaten about the head by the white group which included a number of skinheads... last night he was said to be critical but stable in the Royal London hospital. (*The Guardian,* 10 September 1993)

People like Quaddus Ali have been attacked because they were seen as being 'different' from the white population by virtue of their colour, ethnicity or nationality. Eight people have died in Britain as a result of what are believed to be racially motivated attacks in 1992 (Black to Black no.1 July 1993; CARF Nos. 1-17 1991-1993). A further three people died in 1993. These were Fiaz Mirza, a taxi-driver in east London, Stephen Lawrence, an 18 year-old schoolboy, stabbed whilst waiting at a bus-stop in Eltham, south-east London and Ali Ibrahim in Brighton (CARF 1994: 5). A recent report highlighted the gravity of the situation faced by minority ethnic communities in parts of Britain:

> Reports from monitoring groups, advice centres, and legal officers... told of increasing racist vandalism, graffiti, and personal abuse in the streets, estates and schools. They detailed incidents of black people being forced to leave their homes and businesses because of racist abuse, of families living under self-imposed curfews, and of so-called reception committees springing up to vandalise or deface houses allocated to black families and turn out in force to greet the new tenants. (NCCL 1993: 33)

Recent political developments have served to strengthen such apprehension. Although Britain, unlike parts of Europe, does not have a far-right party of national electoral significance at present (CIRX 1990: 33; Husbands 1994: 563-579), the far-right British National Party (BNP) has managed to secure significant electoral support in a number of socially deprived inner-city wards, particularly in east London.

The election of the BNP candidate, Derek Beackon, in a Millwall ward of the London Borough of Tower Hamlets in September 1993, meant the BNP gained their first seat on a local council since the National Front won two seats in May 1976 in Blackburn (CARF No.17 November/December 1993: 9). Although the BNP lost this seat to the Labour Party in the May 1994 local elections, their candidate came second with 2041 votes, 28 per cent of the total votes cast. The other two BNP candidates in Millwall also received over 25 per cent of the votes. Similarly, in the neighbouring London borough of Newham, the BNP received between 24 per cent and 33 per cent of the votes in the five seats they contested in the local elections (cited in the *New Statesman and Society,* 13 May 1994).

The BNP's electoral support is, however, restricted to specific geographical localities. In the May 1994 local elections there were only three seats outside the east London boroughs of Newham and Tower Hamlets in which they gained over 10 per cent of the votes. Indeed Husbands (1994: 576) contends that what should be of most concern is not the electoral potential of the BNP but rather their physical presence and activities, which help to 'create a local climate facilitating racial violence, so that some of those otherwise merely disposed to indulge in it acquire the confidence for actual perpetration from the BNP's presence'.

It is precisely this physical presence of the BNP coupled with the volume and alarming nature of racial attacks in east London recently, that has resulted in the minority ethnic community feeling particularly vulnerable. However, it is important to emphasise that intimidation has not been the sole consequence of such vulnerability to racial violence and harassment. Many have actively sought to address the problem using a number of approaches.

These have included making strong demands to local councils and the police to tackle the problem more effectively. There has been some institutional response including in the east London borough of Tower Hamlets, where the council established a 24-hour racial harassment hotline. This confidential information service enables residents to pass on information about racist activities in the local area which can then be investigated by the council (MR and AMA News: April 1994: 29). Similarly, it is commonly believed that the rise in racially motivated attacks reported to the police in east London is an indication, in part at least, of the greater willingness of the victims to report such criminal activity and of the police in recording it. This important issue will be discussed more fully in Chapter 2.

On the other hand, some members of the minority ethnic community have sought redress by going to local anti-racist groups who provide advice and support to people who have suffered from racial violence and harassment. There are many such groups in east London, reflecting the widespread concern amongst the minority ethnic community about the problem. They include the Newham Monitoring Project (NMP) which has been undertaking such work for the past fifteen years; the Greenwich Action Committee Against Racial Attacks (GACARA); the Campaign Against Racism and Fascism (CARF), an umbrella organisation for several local groups throughout the country. The recent period has also witnessed the establishment of self-defence groups, especially in those localities where the BNP has been active. One such group is Shadwell Community Defence (SCD) which was established to protect local South Asians under threat from racial violence from the BNP in a recent local council by-election in September 1994.

It was the concern felt in some quarters of the wider community at the nature and extent of racial violence and harassment that was taking place, particularly in east London, coupled with the presence of the BNP in this area, and the belief that it may be the precursor to racial violence elsewhere in the country, that played an important part in the establishment of two national anti-racist organisations in 1991: the Anti-Nazi League (ANL) and the Anti-Racist Alliance (ARA). These organisations have adopted different though complementary strategies in addressing the problem in Britain.

The re-established Anti-Nazi League (ANL) has held meetings and established local branches throughout the country comprising all who wish to campaign against fascism and racism. The central objective underpinning this strategy is the belief that only by organising the greatest number of people (including both ethnic minorities and white people) to demonstrate their active opposition to fascism and racism, and thereby creating a climate of public opinion in Britain that is unfavourable to them, can the rise of fascism be prevented. This strategy has been used to mobilise people on several occasions. The demonstration calling for the closure of the BNP bookshop in Welling in October 1993 was organised jointly by members of the ANL and Youth Against Racism in Europe (YRE) – another anti-nazi group. Similarly, 100,000 people – the biggest anti-racist gathering in Britain since the Rock Against Racism carnival at Victoria Park in East London in May 1978 (Gilroy 1987: 132) – attended a march and festival on Saturday 28 May 1994 to demonstrate their opposition to fascism and racism in Britain (cited in the *Observer,* 29 May 1994).

While the ANL mainly seeks to tackle the threat from organised fascism, the Anti-Racist Alliance (ARA) has a wider remit – tackling everyday racism as well as organised fascism. The organisation lays particular emphasis on black self-organisation, a strategy which, they believe, allows African Caribbean and South Asians to take the lead in setting the agenda in how the problem ought to be addressed. In addition to organising demonstrations against racism and fascism, ARA have also devoted their energies to pressing Parliament to introduce legislation to deal with racial violence and harassment. A recent report by the Anti-Racist Alliance national conference in Greenwich (1993) highlighted the case for a racial harassment bill as one way of curbing the problem.

The roles of the ANL and ARA have come under some criticism. There has been some concern about the relationship between these single-issue campaigns and both mainstream and militant political parties. Concern has also been expressed about whether violence should be confronted with violence whilst nevertheless recognising that a response is needed.

Several parliamentary committees and government departments have also undertaken initiatives to address the problem. Since the problem was first placed on the policy agenda in 1981, it has been the subject of several reports. In 1986, the House of Commons Home Affairs Committee report on racial attacks and harassment (1986) noted that 'the most shameful and dispiriting aspect of race relations in Britain is the incidence of racial attacks and harassment'. It recommended that a multi-agency approach be adopted, that is, one which co-ordinated the efforts of all the different agencies having an interest in tackling the problem. A major report by the Inter-Departmental Racial Attacks Group (1989) then laid down extensive guidelines on how best to move towards using such a co-ordinated approach. This initiative was quickly followed by a second report by the Inter-Departmental Racial Attacks Group in 1991 which evaluated how far its recommendations had been implemented and also provided examples of best practice.

The Department of the Environment published a good practice guide for local authorities on tackling racial violence and harassment of council tenants (1989). In 1991, they followed this up by undertaking a postal survey of all local housing authorities in England and Wales to examine to what extent racial violence and harassment was seen as a problem locally and to assess the impact and effectiveness of the good practice guide produced by the department and the first report of the Inter-Departmental Racial Attacks Group, both of which had been sent out to local authorities in 1989. Thirty-eight of the 85 local authorities that responded thought that racial violence and harassment was a 'serious' or 'very serious' problem in their area. The Department of the Environment also found that most authorities had seen and acted upon the department's good practice guide. The report went on to make a number of recommendations including encouraging all local authorities to review their policies and procedures on racial violence and harassment to ensure they were in line with the department's good practice guide. They also encouraged local authorities to adopt a common definition of racial violence and harassment to ensure the effective working of the multi-agency approach (Love and Kirby 1994).

The European context

The public concern surrounding the problem of racial violence and harassment (and the resultant reaction to it amongst certain quarters) in Britain cannot be divorced from the context of recent developments in parts of Europe. According to the European Parliament, *'the number of racist attacks across the 12 community states rose by between 5 and 10 per cent in the late 1980s'* (cited in Skellington and Morris 1992: 61). Many people in Britain watched on television the events that unfolded in Rostock, Germany, in August 1992 when bands of nazis, armed with petrol bombs, launched an orchestrated attack against reception centres for asylum seekers.

Germany, partly as a result of its recent historical past, has been the country where concern surrounding the issue of racial violence has been particularly highlighted with extensive coverage in the German media of serious racial attacks directed against minorities in the past three years. There were 2600 recorded racially-motivated attacks on 'foreigners' in the period from January 1991 to October 1992 of which 1200 took place during the first month of 1992 (Kohl 1993: 151). Twenty-five people died in 1992 (CARF No. 18 1994 Jan/ Feb. p.4) and a further 12 people died in the first three months of 1993 'in incidents that can either be proved to be racially motivated or where a racial motive cannot be ruled out' (Fekete 1993: 163).

Similarly, France has also been witness to serious cases of racial violence. Indeed, a new word 'Arabcide' has been coined to describe the widespread violence against North Africans that resulted in the death of eight people in 1992 (Fekete 1992: 162). The 1989 report of the *'Commission Nationale des Droits de l'homme'*, distinguishing between 'actions' covering assault, shooting, arson and damage to property, and 'threats' covering graffiti, leaflets and telephone calls, found that 'actions' had remained fairly stable at 46-70 reported incidents a year in the past decade. On the other hand, 'threats', which had been stable throughout the mid-1980s at 100 reported incidents per year, had increased to 135 in 1988 and to 237 in 1989 (cited in Oakley 1992: 24). However, the extent of the problem has not been fully reflected in the number of racially motivated incidents reported to the police. An alternative picture of racial violence and harassment in France in the past decade was shown by a poll undertaken by the anti-racist organisation MRAP, which found that 7 per cent of ethnic minorities had been physically attacked; 6 per cent had been pushed about and 30 per cent had been verbally abused in a public place (cited in Oakley 1992: 24).

Such acts of racial violence and harassment in Europe have not been restricted to people of colour alone. The 'old racisms' have also re-emerged recently: several Jewish cemeteries have been desecrated with racist graffiti in both France and Germany (Oakley 1992; ICCLA 1993 and the Institute of Jewish Affairs 1994).

It should be noted that comparison of the nature and scale of the problem across the various European states is difficult for two related reasons. Firstly, definitions as to what constitutes an act of racial violence and harassment differ markedly between countries and sometimes within countries: in Germany, the security service collect data only on physical attacks whereas in Britain, the police use a broader definition that in theory seeks to capture incidents of 'low level' harassment that are reported to them. On the other hand, in Sweden, data is collected only on what are referred to as 'terrorist attacks'. The second difficulty relating to comparison across the European states is that the targets of such racial violence and harassment are different in each country. Hence, in Britain, the overwhelming majority of victims tend to be South Asians and African Caribbeans whereas in Germany they are people of Turkish origin. On the other hand, in eastern Europe, the victims of such violence tend to be white ethnic minorities like Jews and Gypsies. (For a fuller discussion of these issues, see Bjorgo and Witte 1993: Chapter 1.)

Nevertheless, accounts of racial violence and harassment are to be found in most other countries of western Europe and are regularly reported in the daily press (for more information, see Fekete 1993; CARF Nos. 1-22, 1991-1994; *The Guardian*, 6 February 1993 and *Race and Class*, Vol.32 No.3 1991). The Campaign Against Racism and Fascism (CARF) (1994: 5) counted 59 racially-motivated murders in Western Europe in 1993 and claimed to have found evidence that the far-right had been directly implicated in 43 of them.[1] Of these 59 racially-motivated murders, 17 were of children under the age of 15 (CARF 1994: 8). Oakley (1992: 40) has concluded that 'there is prima facie (if often anecdotal) evidence that racial violence and harassment occur in all countries of Europe in which visible minorities of post-war immigrant origin are settled'.

The problem has been recognised by the European Parliament which has published three major reports on the rise of racism and xenophobia in Europe in the past decade. These include the report by the Committee of Inquiry into fascism and racism in Europe, commonly referred to as the

Evrigenis report of 1985; a report by the Committee of Inquiry into Racism and Xenophobia (CIRX) in 1990, commonly referred to as the Ford Report; and a report by the Committee on Civil Liberties and Internal Affairs (CCLIA) in 1993. In addition, the Council of Europe has also published a report looking at racial violence and harassment in Europe (Oakley 1992).

Such racial violence and harassment, although not always directly attributable, cannot be divorced from the growth of far-right electoral parties across some countries of western Europe for the first time since the end of the second world war. It is evident that the far-right is now a significant political force in many countries. A report by the Committee on Civil Liberties and Internal Affairs (CCLIA) in 1993 on the resurgence of racism and xenophobia in Europe and the danger of extremist far-right violence recognised this fact and sought to draw

> attention to the proliferation in the Member States of extreme right-wing groups, parties and movements – some of which are organised and maintain links with each other – which have in common an 'ideology' based on racist and anti-Semitic attitudes, leading them to commit acts of violence, acts of vandalism of every kind against Community and non-Community citizens, refugees, asylum-seekers, gypsies, Jews, and other minority groups and exploit a situation of social discontent and disarray to incite others particularly young people – to racial hatred by blaming 'foreigners' for current economic problems and the rise in unemployment (CCLIA 1993: 5)

A brief review of recent electoral results in some of the key countries of western Europe demonstrates the relative strength of such far-right parties. It shows that electoral support for the far-right is uneven and varies across countries with some having quite substantial support whilst in others it remains minimal.

In France, the far-right party, the Front National, has been an important political force for almost a decade. It received 12.5 per cent of the vote in the March 1993 general election although no seats in Parliament. It had 239 councillors elected across France since the 1992 local elections. The report by the Committee of Inquiry into Racism and Xenophobia (CIRX) in 1990 estimated that the FN had a membership of 100,000 and a further 200,000 sympathisers. The recent European elections held in June 1994 showed that although its vote had declined slightly from 12 per cent to 10 per cent they had held on to all their 10 seats in the European Parliament.

However, it is in Italy that the far-right have scored their biggest success to date. The general election in Italy in March 1994 resulted in the victory of the far-right in the form of the Freedom Alliance. The three parties that made up this alliance, Silvio Berlusconi's Forza Italia, Umberto Bossi's Northern League, and Gianfranco Fini's National Alliance, won over 50 per cent of the vote and a majority of seats in both houses of Parliament (cited in the *New Statesman and Society*, 1 April 1994, p.10). The victory of this coalition meant that the fascists, in the form of Fini's National Alliance (formerly the Movimento Sociale Italiano (MSI), Mussolini's party) won a share of power for the first time since the fall of Mussolini in 1943. This coalition government has since fallen. The June 1994 European election confirmed the strong support for the Freedom Alliance with the fascist National Alliance doubling its share of the vote from 6 per cent in 1989 to 13 per cent. This meant that it now had 11 seats in the European Parliament compared to four in 1989.

In Belgium, the far-right Vlaams Blok, campaigning on the slogan of 'our own people first', won 12 seats in the Chamber of Representatives, five seats in the Senate, and 6.6 per cent of the national vote in the 1991 elections. The June 1994 European election results suggested that the Vlaams Blok had further consolidated its support. It received 7 per cent of the vote and two seats. A second far-right party in Belgium, the National Front, received 3 per cent of the vote and gained its first European parliamentary seat.

On the other hand, some far-right parties have witnessed a decline in electoral support. In the immediate two years that followed German re-unification, the far-right Republikaner Party succeeded in gaining a significant share of the electoral vote. In the April 1992 elections, they gained 11 per cent of the total vote and 15 seats in the state government. However, the June 1994 European elections saw their share of the vote decline from 7 per cent in 1989 to 4 per cent. In terms of seats, this meant they lost all six seats they had previously held from the 1989 European elections.

Similarly, in the Netherlands, the far-right party, Centrum Demokraten, has failed to achieve an electoral breakthrough. It received only minimal electoral support and its vote fell from 3 per cent in the last European elections in 1989 to 1 per cent in 1994.

The appearance of far-right electoral parties has not been restricted to parts of western Europe. The rise of ethnic-specific political parties has accompanied the 'ethnic cleansing' going on in the former nation state of Yugoslavia. Elsewhere in eastern Europe, the collapse of Stalinism has been accompanied by the growth of political parties that are increasingly and openly anti-semitic and anti-Gypsy. The CCLIA report (1993: 5) highlighted

> that the countries of Eastern Europe, whose young, still fragile democracies are particularly susceptible to the dangers of an authoritarian backlash, have also witnessed the emergence of extreme right-wing organisations and are experiencing a marked increase in racist, xenophobic and anti-semitic tendencies.

Some of the far-right parties in eastern Europe that have managed to achieve some relative electoral success are as follows. The Slovak National Party entered the coalition government in March 1994. The Hungarian Democratic Forum is the largest partner in the present coalition government (for more information on these developments see Fekete 1993: 159-168; Oakley 1992; CCLIA 1993 and CARF 1994: No.20: 2). Perhaps of most concern is the Liberal Democratic Party of Russia led by Vladimir Zhirinovsky, which, in the general election of December 1993, secured 23 per cent of the popular vote, making it the largest political party in Russia. *(The Guardian,* 31 December 1993).

Overview of this report

These related developments have contributed to creating an unprecedented level of public debate recently about the problem of racial violence and harassment in many parts of Europe (Bjorgo and Witte 1993). A related corollary of this heightened concern and awareness has been the belief that the recent period has been witness to an increase in levels of racial violence and harassment. This view has existed both in relation to mainland Europe (Ford 1992) and Britain (ARA 1993; Parekh 1994; Home Affairs Select Committee 1994). However, others have questioned the assumption that there has been an increase in the scale of the problem, arguing that such a view fails to reflect the wide variation in the size of the problem across the different countries of Europe (Miles 1994).

For the purposes of this study, it was decided that the definition proposed by the CRE in their study of racial violence and harassment in local housing estates (CRE 1987:8) would serve the purpose of investigating the full range of the problem. This states:

> Racial harassment is violence which may be verbal or physical and which includes attacks on property as well as on the person, suffered by individuals or groups because of their colour, race, nationality or ethnic or national origins, when the victim believes that the perpetrator was acting on racial grounds and/or there is evidence of racism.

This definition has the advantage of allowing incidents of 'low level' racial harassment such as racial abuse to be included in addition to racial attacks and racially motivated damage to property.

Chapter 2 will review existing statistics and research to examine the scale of the problem in Britain and establish whether it has increased. The objective of investigating the scale of the problem is to provide a more accurate measure in order to improve our understanding of the phenomenon and to enable it to be tackled more effectively.

Chapter 3 of the report presents the findings from a new qualitative study based on depth interviews with 74 African Caribbean and South Asian people which explored the nature of the different forms of racial violence and harassment and in particular gathered more information on aspects of 'low-level' racial harassment.

Chapter 4 of the report is also based on the qualitative study and examines briefly another often neglected aspect of the problem – the 'hidden injuries of racism' – that is, how the lives of African Caribbean and South Asian people are affected beyond the actual racial violence and harassment that takes place.

The report concludes with a discussion of the key issues involved in addressing the problem more effectively.

Note

1. CARF claim to have found evidence that a further 16 deaths occurred as a result of 'police brutality' and 'suicide provoked by official racism' (CARF No.18 January/ February 1994).

2 Racial violence and harassment in Britain: assessing the evidence

Introduction
The developments that have been outlined in the introduction make it more pertinent than ever to investigate the levels of racial violence and harassment in Britain. Fortunately, Britain has access to two national data sets which provide information on the scale of the problem. These are racial incidents that are reported to the police and a victimisation survey called the British Crime Survey (BCS). Each of these data sets is analysed in this chapter to see what insights they provide. Furthermore, to investigate how accurate their estimation of the scale of the problem is, the problems associated with each of them are fully discussed. This will include a critical examination of how each data set has defined and sought to measure levels of racial violence and harassment.

The chapter then moves on to a third source of information on racial violence and harassment – a series of 'special' surveys and studies undertaken (using a variety of methods) in different local areas. Although this source of information cannot provide a reliable estimate of the overall scale of the problem in Britain, some of the findings from these studies do raise a number of key points which are of importance if we are to understand the nature of the phenomenon. In particular, the discussion will centre around two key themes which require more thorough investigation: whether there is geographical variation in levels of racial violence and harassment by area (and relatedly minority ethnic concentration) and the nature of repeat victimisation.

The police and racial violence and harassment
Although racial violence is a phenomenon that has existed within Britain since at least the end of World War One (Fryer 1984), the problem only recently arrived on the political agenda. According to Gordon (1993: 168-169), three factors were important in placing it there. These were the number of deaths of minority ethnic people that occurred in 1980-81 as a result of racial violence; the response of the minority ethnic communities

in establishing self-defence groups to protect their communities from such violence, which Gordon claims were seen 'by those in power as a threat to public order'; and the publication of a report by the Joint Committee Against Racialism (JCAR) in 1980 which brought to the attention of the government the widespread concern that existed in society about racial violence. In response to these developments, the government established a Home Office working party to investigate the scale of racial violence in Britain. The report, entitled *Racial Attacks,* was published by the Home Office in 1981. The report's findings were based on a survey undertaken in England and Wales of 13 police areas looking at 'inter-racial' incidents reported to the police. An 'inter-racial' incident was defined as one 'where the victim was of a different ethnic origin from the suspect or alleged offender'. These 'inter-racial' incidents were then analysed by Home Office researchers to identify those particular incidents they considered to be racially motivated.

The study found that the rate of racially motivated victimisation was 1.4 per 100,000 population for whites; 51.2 per 100,000 population for African Caribbeans; and 69.7 per 100,000 population for South Asians. Hence, the study showed that South Asians were 50 times more likely than whites to be victims of racially motivated incidents and African Caribbeans 36 times more likely (Home Office 1981: 10-11). On the basis of this evidence, the report estimated that there were 7,000 racially motivated incidents reported to police forces in England and Wales in one year. The 1981 study was replicated by the Home Office in 1987 using the same 13 police areas. The rate of racially motivated victimisation was found to be 0.5 per 100,000 population for whites; 21.3 per 100,000 population for African Caribbeans; and 70.3 per 100,000 population for South Asians. Consequently, the study showed that the rate of racially motivated victimisation had remained broadly the same for South Asians but had declined significantly for African Caribbeans (Seagrave 1989: 20).

Although both studies confirmed that ethnic minorities were more likely to suffer from racially motivated crime than whites, concern was expressed about how the police had conceptualised and defined the problem (Gordon 1990; 1993 and Oakley 1992). These authors contended that it was the element of racial motivation that was the key to understanding the exact nature of racial violence and harassment. Oakley (1992: 11) asserted that:

> The distinguishing feature of *racial* violence and harassment is not simply that it involves members of different racial groups or ethnic groups: it is that the action is racially *motivated...* Racially-motivated behaviour, therefore, is not an attack aimed at a person purely as an individual, but an attack on a member of a category or group.

The police were criticised for failing to recognise this important distinction in their definition and for continuing to subsume attacks where the motivation was the victim's 'race' or colour within the broad category of 'inter-racial incidents' which encompassed all criminal incidents involving members of different ethnic groups. Hence, a burglary committed by a black man against a white household (where the motivation was to steal) would be recorded as an inter-racial incident just as an attack on a black youth (directed at him because of his colour) by a group of white skinheads. As Gordon (1990:5) writes

> How racial attacks are defined is not, therefore, an academic point but one with serious practical consequences, since it is only by recognising the nature of racially-motivated attacks on black people that one can begin to tackle the problem. To confuse such attacks with ordinary criminal attacks, or to claim, in the absence of any evidence, that attacks by black people on white people are 'racial' is to render the concept of racism quite meaningless.

To highlight this distinct form of violence and harassment directed at people because they are seen as 'racially different', some have sought to substitute the term 'racist violence and harassment' for racial violence and harassment. This debate can be explored in Kimber and Cooper (1991) and Gordon (1992 and 1993).

The intention of this discussion about how a racial incident has been defined by the police has not been to rule out the possibility that some white people can be victims of racial violence and harassment. There is ample evidence of racial violence directed against white minority ethnic groups such as the Irish dating from the middle of the nineteenth century (Thompson 1991: 469-485); and against Jews since the 1930s (Beckman 1993; the Institute of Jewish Affairs 1994) and, more recently against white partners in mixed 'race' relationships (Fitzgerald and Ellis 1989). Nevertheless, it remains the case that the overwhelming proportion of victims of racial violence and harassment in Britain today are the 'visible minorities'.

The police have sought to address some of the criticisms that have been levelled at them, including modifying how they define a racially motivated incident. A standard definition of a racial incident put forward by the Association of Chief Police Officers (ACPO) was adopted by all the police forces of England and Wales in 1985. According to this definition, a racial incident constituted 'any incident in which it appears to the reporting or investigating officer that the complaint involves an element of racial motivation; or any incident which includes an allegation of racial motivation made by the person'.

However, this definition has also come under recent criticism, including from the ACPO themselves in the form of Paul Whitehouse, Chief Constable of Sussex Police. During questioning by the Home Affairs Select Committee (1994: Vol.2: 16) he acknowledged the 'subjective' nature of the definition and the possibility that it could capture incidents involving minority ethnic and white people that were not racially motivated. Peter Lloyd, the then Minister of State at the Home Office, also acknowledged this difficulty with the police definition but contended that it did have the important attribute of placing the emphasis of racial motivation on the victim's perception and thereby indicating the agency's support for the victim.

With these criticisms in mind, it is to the statistics of incidents of racial violence and harassment reported to the police that we now turn to investigate what they tell us about the scale of the problem in Britain.

The scale of the problem: racial incidents reported to the police

The number of racial incidents reported to the police over the period of 1988 to 1993 are shown in Table 1.

Table 1   Number of reported racial incidents in England and Wales

	1988	1989	1990	1991	1992	1993/94
Provinces	2169	2347	3451	4509	4507	5873
Metropolitan Police	2214	2697	2908	3373	3227	3889
England and Wales	4383	5044	6359	7882	7734	9762

(Table derived from *Hansard,* 26 April 1993 and *Hansard,* 24 June 1994.)

*   Since 1993 the information has been collected on a financial year basis rather than a calendar year basis as in previous years. However, the figures have been collected by the same means as before and remain comparable.

As shown by Table 1, racially motivated incidents reported to the police have risen in England and Wales from 4,383 in 1988 to 9,762 in 1993/94, an increase of 123 per cent over five years (although there was a slight decrease between 1991 and 1992). A large number of these incidents occurred in the Greater London area. In 1993/94, for example, 40 per cent of all racially motivated incidents reported to the police occurred in Greater London. However, this can be explained by the distribution of the minority ethnic population of which 45 per cent live in the Greater London area according to the 1991 census.

On the basis of these racially motivated incidents reported to the police it would be understandable for people to conclude that there was an increase in the level of racial violence and harassment over the period of 1988 to 1993/94 in Britain. However, such police statistics need to be treated with great caution (see for example the discussion in Bottomley and Pease 1993). It is well established that the real level of crime is not accurately reflected in statistics recorded by the police (Mayhew, Aye Maung and Mirrlees-Black: 1993). This applies equally to statistics collected by the police on racially motivated offences.

There is a large body of evidence to suggest that well over half of all victims of such offences do not report them to the police. For example, the third PSI national survey of minority ethnic groups (Brown 1984) found that 60 per cent of victims did not report such racially motivated incidents to the police. Similarly, data from the 1988 and 1992 British Crime Surveys (discussed in detail below) suggests that this continues to be the case with well over half of both African Caribbeans and South Asians not reporting racially motivated incidents to the police.

Despite these difficulties associated with measuring the real level of racially motivated crime, it should be noted that recent police efforts to encourage victims to report such crimes to them do seem to be having some effect and this might be one factor that explains part of the rise in reported racial incidents. The BCS found that levels of reporting by African Caribbeans and South Asians of racially motivated incidents have increased since 1987. In the 1988 BCS, 27 per cent of all racially motivated offences against African Caribbeans were reported compared to 34 per cent in the 1992 survey. Similarly, levels of reporting racially motivated offences against South Asians rose from 39 per cent in the 1988 BCS to 45 per cent in the 1992 BCS (Aye Maung and Mirrlees-Black 1994: 20). However, an important point to bear in mind is that not all of the racially motivated crimes said to have been reported to the police by the British Crime Survey were actually recorded as such by the official police statistics.

Changes in police statistics may indicate changes in the behaviour of the police and victims as much as rises or falls in the actual number of incidents. For example, it is widely recognised that at least part of the increase in the number of rapes recorded by the police in recent years is a consequence of an increased willingness on the part of some women to report such incidents (Edwards 1994). Thus, it is not possible to accurately conclude from the police statistics that there has been an increase in levels of racial violence and harassment.

It is to the second data set that we must turn to see if it can provide a more accurate estimate of the scale of the problem.

The British Crime Survey (BCS): a more accurate estimate of the problem?

Since 1988, Britain, has had access to an alternative data set on the level of racial violence and harassment, namely the British Crime Survey (BCS). This victimisation survey sets out to establish a more accurate picture of crime by covering people's experience of victimisation over the last year irrespective of whether they have reported it to the police. This helps to establish what is commonly referred to as the 'dark-figure' of crime, that is, the level of unrecorded crime (BCS 1992: 2). The 1988 BCS comprised a nationally representative 'core' sample of 10,392 households aged 16 or older, and an additional 'booster' sample of 1,349 African Caribbeans and South Asians to allow a more reliable picture of the scale of criminal victimisation against them (Mayhew, Elliot and Dowds 1989: 6). The 1992 BCS comprised a nationally representative 'core' sample of 10,059 households and an additional 'booster' sample of 1,654 African Caribbeans and South Asians (Mayhew, Aye Maung and Mirrlees-Black 1993: 7).

The BCS collects information on people's experience of selected crimes and threats. There are two broad categories of crime: incidents in which the household is the primary victim, and those where the individual person is the primary victim. In addition, those South Asian and African Caribbean respondents who said they had been victims of crime were also asked whether they thought any incidents they experienced had been racially motivated.

Both the 1988 and 1992 BCS surveys showed that South Asians and African Caribbeans were at greater risk of being victims of crime than were whites. Although much of this difference in relation to African Caribbeans was explained by social and demographic factors such as age, gender, type of accommodation and area of residence, these factors were not sufficient in explaining the differential rate of victimisation between South Asians and whites, with South Asians remaining at greater risk of certain crimes such as vandalism, robbery and thefts from the person. Hence, Aye Maung and Mirrlees-Black (1994: 8) argued that ethnicity for South Asians 'appear[s] to contribute directly to their higher risks for some crimes'.

Table 2 shows the results from the 1988 and 1992 surveys for the main offences in which a racial element was most often present – assaults, threats and vandalism. It shows that overall there has been no increase in the proportion of racial violence and harassment between 1987 and 1991. In particular, the table shows that the proportion of all offences reported by

Table 2   Per cent of incidents seen as racially motivated: 1988 and 1992 BCS

Type of offence	African Caribbean		South Asian	
	1988	1992	1988	1992
Assault	34	24	36	56
Threats	44	24	50	66
Vandalism	20	23	32	26
All BCS offences	15	13	24	24

Source: 1988 and 1992 BCS core and minority ethnic boost samples weighted data
          table taken from Aye Maung and Mirrlees-Black (1994: 13)

African Caribbeans as being racially motivated declined from 15 per cent in 1988 to 13 per cent in 1992. On the other hand, the proportion of offences reported by South Asians as being racially motivated in 1992 remained the same as in 1988 at 24 per cent. When looking at individual offences, fewer assaults and threats were seen as racially motivated by African Caribbeans whereas more assaults and threats were seen as racially motivated by South Asians.

The BCS also allows estimates to be made of the number of offences of different kinds in 1991 by grossing up survey-based risks of victimisation by the number of adults in the population of England and Wales. By undertaking a similar calculation to estimate the number of incidents against ethnic minorities the BCS concluded that there were approximately 130,000 incidents of crimes and threats against South Asians and African Caribbeans which were thought to be racially motivated. Of these, 89,000 were believed to be against South Asians and 41,000 against African Caribbeans.[1] This represents 18 per cent of the estimated total of 730,000 crimes against them, which in turn represents just under 5 per cent of the total estimate of almost 17 million incidents of criminal victimisation and threats experienced by the national population in England and Wales in 1991 (Aye Maung and Mirrlees-Black 1994: 13-15). Taking account of the number of adults in each group in the population, these figures suggest an annual victimisation rate of 65 incidents per 1,000 African Caribbeans and 95 incidents per 1,000 South Asians. The BCS therefore lends some support to the idea that South Asians are rather more at risk of racially motivated offences than African Caribbeans.

Several important points emerge from these two national data sets regarding the incidence of racial violence and harassment. By covering people's experience of racially motivated crimes irrespective of whether they have been reported to the police, the BCS gives a more accurate picture of the scale of the problem. The BCS estimated that there had been a total of 130,000 racially motivated crimes against South Asians and African Caribbeans. This greatly exceeds the estimates based on racial incidents reported to the police. The BCS therefore suggests that although the level of racial violence and harassment has been steadier than the police statistics demonstrated, the overall number of incidents throughout the period has been far higher than people had realised.

Problems associated with victimisation surveys

Although the estimate provided by the BCS is a more accurate measure of the scale of the problem than racial incidents reported to the police, it remains only a partial picture of the scale of racial violence and harassment in Britain. The BCS examines only incidents of racial violence and harassment that are criminal (Mayhew, Elliot and Dowds 1989: 41). It does not cover what is commonly referred to as 'low-level' racial harassment such as racial abuse and other types of insulting behaviour which though not technically criminal constitute an important form of racial violence and harassment.

Furthermore, victimisation surveys like the BCS have also come under criticism for a number of other reasons. Hesse et al (1992) have argued that although these surveys are able to provide firmer evidence on the extent of particular crimes, they are not capable by themselves of giving a detailed and fully-rounded picture of the nature of racial violence and harassment and its underlying causes. This is because of

> the incapacity of the crime survey to capture victimisation experiences which are processual, that is regular occurrences; they simply cannot quantify this. The cyclical and multiple features of particular forms of victimisation are therefore not reflected in crime surveys. (Hesse et al 1992: 160)

As a result, a victimisation survey reduces what is really a pattern of repeat victimisation to apparently isolated acts of racial hostility devoid of any social context or location in time (Hesse 1992 and Bowling 1993). This 'events-oriented approach' runs the risk of failing to capture those acts of 'low-level' racial harassment that form part of an integral and on-going process of victimisation which serves to create a climate of continuous insecurity for the victims.

Hesse et al (1992) in their important study *Beneath the Surface: Racial Harassment* attempted to address this failing of victimisation surveys by adopting a different methodological approach for studying racial harassment in the London Borough of Waltham Forest. By establishing a

Council Panel of Inquiry and adopting a case study methodology they were able to seek the views of local residents, both victims and perpetrators, and representatives from the local council, community and housing groups as well as drawing on evidence provided by the police (Hesse et al 1992: 221-226). The result was a fully-contextualised report that sought to explain not only the extent and nature of the problem but also the critical local factors that played a part in giving rise to it.[2]

On the other hand, Bowling (1993: 245) although welcoming such an innovative approach to the study of racial violence and harassment has suggested that a potential danger of a solely qualitative method is that it may be thought of as being 'unscientific or actually failing to bring sufficient rigour to the collection and analysis of data'. Instead he put forward the proposition that seeks to marry the two approaches by calling for victimisation surveys to be an essential component of all case study analysis of racial harassment. Similarly, Fitzgerald and Ellis (1989: 60) have proposed that surveys:

> should be complemented by qualitative and quantitative information generated through in-depth interviews. Together, both qualitative and quantitative information need to be interpreted within a social (and even historical) perspective which takes account of variations in local circumstances.

'Special' surveys on racial violence and harassment

The third source of information on racial violence and harassment that exists in Britain is a series of 'special' surveys and studies that have been undertaken to measure the scale of the problem in different areas. Apart from one national survey, these studies are unable to provide insights into the scale of the overall problem in Britain. However, they are useful in allowing a discussion of some key issues concerning the problem, including whether there is variation in levels of racial violence and harassment by area, the nature of repeat victimisation and identifying those aspects of the problem that require further investigation.

The only national survey of this type was the third PSI survey on minority ethnic groups (Brown 1984) which sought to measure the extent of racial violence indirectly by looking at two types of crime victimisation: physical attacks and damage to property.

After inspecting the detailed description of all incidents of physical attack reported by respondents, Brown separated those incidents which were 'inter-racial' in nature, that is, those where Asians or West Indians had been attacked by whites and where whites had been attacked by Asians or West Indians. These inter-racial incidents were then further sub-divided into three categories which comprised:

- incidents where the victim specifically mentioned a racial motive, a racialist organisation or an obvious background of racial hostility.

- incidents where the attack was apparently unprovoked and where no motive was stated or apparent from the description.

- incidents where a racial motive was not involved, in the judgement of the researcher (based upon the description provided), or where the victim stated that no racial motive was involved.

The total sample of 4835 people were asked whether they had been attacked over the past 16-18 month period prior to the interview. Brown found ten cases of physical attack where a racial motive was specifically mentioned by the victim; 18 incidents of which the large number were clearly racist in nature, and a further 28 incidents where the researcher or the victim adjudged there was no racial motive involved (Brown 1984: 260, Table 134). He estimated that even if only half the incidents falling in category b, were counted as racial attacks, the actual frequency of racial attacks was still ten times that estimated by the 1981 Home Office study. That is, the PSI estimate of the total number of racial attacks was 70,000.

Most of the special surveys have sought to be more inclusive, and have tried to cover 'low-level' racial harassment as well as criminal offences. One key point to emerge from these surveys has been the considerable variation in levels of racial violence and harassment by area.

A survey undertaken for a Home Office funded pilot multi-agency project in Newham, East London in 1988 found that between one in five and one in six African Caribbean and South Asian men and women suffered a racial incident in an 18 month period (21 per cent and 17 per cent of African Caribbean women and men respectively, and 18 per cent and 19 per cent of South Asian women and men, respectively). Eight per cent of the white men and 7 per cent of the white women interviewed in the survey also said they had experienced a racial incident (Saulsbury and Bowling 1991: 119).

A study undertaken by the Preston Borough Council (1992) found a greater prevalence of racial harassment. The study showed that three out of four minority ethnic households in the sample had experienced racial harassment in the past two years. As the report noted (Chahal 1992: 20) the 'level of response indicates quite clearly that the phenomenon of racial harassment is a reality for the majority of minority ethnic people in the borough of Preston'.

The London Housing Survey (1993) undertaken with a total sample size of 6,500 households, including 1,000 minority ethnic households, sought to examine the prevalence of racial violence and harassment in the context of a more general survey of housing circumstances and needs. On the basis of their findings, the authors estimated that 48,000 minority ethnic households had suffered some form of racial harassment in or near their present accommodation. This is a total of one in 14 of all minority ethnic households across the capital, rising to one in 11 for South Asian households. One in ten children from a minority ethnic group were living in a household that had been harassed at home. Of those households that said they had suffered from some form of racial harassment, 25 per cent had been physically attacked; 20 per cent had had their property damaged and two-thirds had been verbally abused because of their colour. It should be noted that when the London Housing Survey asked questions on harassment, they put no time limit on people's experiences because 'one act of violence, however long ago, can still leave a household feeling under threat' (LHS 1993: 2). On the other hand, they only asked about people's experience of harassment whilst in their present home. Hence, these findings should be treated with some caution.

The possible explanations for such variation in levels of racial violence and harassment in different studies have been the subject of much debate (Fitzgerald and Ellis 1989). It is commonly believed that part of the explanation for such a variation is the variety of methods used to collect the data. However, evidence from a Department of the Environment study indicated that it may also reflect real variations in the levels of racial violence and harassment in different areas.

The Department of the Environment study was based upon 200 interviews with a quota sample of African Caribbean, South Asian and white council tenants in each of six selected local authority areas. The study found that the racial harassment of South Asian households varied from 10 per cent in one local authority to 28 per cent in another. Similarly, for African Caribbean households, the level of racial harassment varied from 4 per cent in one local authority to 22 per cent in another (Fitzgerald and Ellis 1989: 53 and Fitzgerald 1989: 7-12).

The difficulties in properly capturing cases of repeat victimisation through survey techniques have already been discussed. The findings from a qualitative study highlight why repeat victimisation is a key aspect of the problem that requires further investigation. A Home Office study (1992) undertaken in an east London estate showed that two in three minority ethnic families suffered repeat victimisation. The study found that 23 Bengali and Somali families had suffered a total of 136 incidents of racial harassment in a six-month period. This included six families who had suffered extremely high levels of repeat victimisation ranging from 12 to 27 incidents in this six-month period. The most heavily victimised family was harassed once every nine days on average (Sampson and Phillips 1992: 5-6).

Similarly high levels of repeat victimisation were recorded in two other studies. Saulsbury and Bowling (1991) recorded a total of 724 incidents amongst the 114 respondents who had experienced some form of racial harassment in an eighteen month period.[3] The types of racial violence and harassment

> ranged from insulting behaviour and threats to assaults, property damage and arson... There were a very large number of 'less serious' incidents and many 'very serious' ones. Some appeared to be one-off events while others were said to be part of a pattern of repeated attacks and harassment. (Saulsbury and Bowling 1992: 118)

The Preston Borough Council survey (1992) also revealed evidence of repeat victimisation. The study found 276 minority ethnic households identifying a total of 628 separate incidents of racial harassment over a two-year period.

The notion that high levels of racial violence and harassment are a phenomenon that is restricted to particular areas of high minority ethnic concentration may also need to be questioned. Since most studies examining the problem of racial violence and harassment have looked at areas with a relatively high minority ethnic concentration it has been automatically assumed that racial violence and harassment was not a problem in areas of low or medium minority ethnic concentration. As Fitzgerald and Ellis (1989: 59) have noted:

> Areas selected for research have tended to be those with high levels of reported harassment and where the victim population is sufficiently numerous to be surveyed without too much difficulty. The common coincidence of these two criteria, though means that isolated minorities living in areas of low concentration have tended to be overlooked although... such groups may be even more at risk.

Certainly, there is some anecdotal evidence emerging to suggest that racial violence and harassment is also a problem in areas of low minority ethnic concentration (Jay 1992; Norwich and Norfolk Racial Equality Council 1994). The report by the Commission for Racial Equality on racial violence and harassment in the south-west of England found

> reports of Asian families having been forced to leave their homes and businesses because of hostility from other villagers; in three cases, their premises had been repeatedly vandalised. In both Devon and Cornwall, restaurant owners and workers have experienced racial abuse and threats, or have had graffiti scrawled on the walls of their premises. (Jay 1992: 18)

Similarly, a study undertaken in the town of Harlow in Essex which has a relatively small minority ethnic population found several incidents of racial harassment including one where

> a woman, newly-working in a large retail establishment, explained how she used to be regularly abused by an old woman as she made her way to work in the mornings, calling her names and telling her to 'go back to Pakistan'. (Wrench, Brar and Martin 1993: 108)

The scale and nature of racial violence and harassment against minority ethnic people in areas of low and medium concentration is a problem that certainly requires more thorough investigation.

Summary
There are two national data sets which provide information on levels of racial violence and harassment in Britain. The first of these, statistics of racial incidents, show an increase in the numbers reported to the police in the past five years; but this is likely to reflect a welcome change in the response to racial harassment by the police rather than an (unwelcome) change in the frequency of the problem. Therefore, this data set cannot provide an accurate measure of the scale of the problem.

The second data set which provides information on levels of racial violence and harassment is the British Crime Survey (BCS). This provides a more accurate picture of the scale of the problem by covering people's experience of racially motivated crime irrespective of whether it has been reported to the police. The survey estimated there had been a total of 130,000 racially motivated crimes against South Asians and African Caribbeans in 1991, comprising 89,000 against South Asians and 41,000 against African Caribbeans. This greatly exceeds the estimate of 7782 reported racial incidents to the police in 1991. The BCS indicated only a slight increase in the number of racially motivated crimes between 1987 and 1991. The BCS therefore suggests that, although the level of racial violence and harassment has been steadier than statistics of racial incidents reported to the police indicated, the overall number of incidents throughout the period has been far higher than people had realised.

Although the estimate provided by the BCS is the most accurate to date, it remains very much a partial picture of the scale of the problem in Britain today because it fails to cover what is commonly referred to as 'low-level' racial harassment. Relatedly, some people have questioned whether victimisation surveys such as the BCS are capable of providing a fully-rounded picture of the nature of racial violence and harassment. It is contended that such surveys reduce what is a process of repeat victimisation to one of discrete acts of racial harassment devoid of any social context.

Hence it has been suggested that more innovative approaches to the problem are required that seek to marry the advantages of both quantitative and qualitative methods if a comprehensive understanding of the problem is to be achieved.

A third source of information on the extent and nature of racial violence and harassment are several 'special' surveys that have been undertaken in different local areas. Although these surveys do not provide a reliable estimate of the national scale of the problem in Britain, they do suggest that levels of racial violence and harassment vary by area. Furthermore, evidence from these studies also suggest that more research needs to be directed towards examining the extent and nature of racial violence and harassment experienced by people who live in areas of low and medium minority ethnic concentration and the extent to which people are subject to repeat victimisation.

Notes

1. About a quarter of the 130,000 estimated incidents were assaults and two-fifths were threats. Vandalism comprised another fifth of the total (Aye Maung and Mirrlees-Black 1994: vi).

2. Two other recent studies have attempted a case study method of inquiry into racial violence and harassment. These are *Sagaland: Youth culture, racism and education,* 1992), a study undertaken in Thamesmead following the racist murder of Rolan Adams which examined the local factors which led a gang of white youths to take such an action, and *Through patterns not our own* (1993), a report based upon a combination of surveys and interviews with caseworkers, looking at the problem of racial violence and harassment on council estates in east London.

3. However, Bowling argues that respondents may not have been correct about the number of times they were victimised for three reasons: firstly, they may not be able to recall the number and nature of incidents accurately over a period of 18 months; secondly, because there was no common definition of racial harassment, some respondents may have defined incidents as racial when the motivation was debatable, or when they could not even be certain that a person from another racial group was responsible for the incident; and finally, others may have ignored incidents they regarded as minor or unimportant (Bowling unpublished: 7).

3 The nature of racial violence and harassment: some findings from a qualitative study

Introduction

We saw earlier that an important weakness of previous national research in the area of racial violence and harassment has been the failure to provide a comprehensive picture of the different forms that racial violence and harassment can take. The BCS sweeps of 1987 and 1991 and PSI's third national survey on minority ethnic groups (Brown 1984) only examined the extent of racially motivated crime. As a result, 'low-level' racial harassment in the form of racial abuse and other forms of insulting and intimidating behaviour were neglected. This form of racial harassment if it persists over a long period of time might be equally serious as physical attacks.

This chapter presents the findings from a qualitative study which sought to explore fully the nature of each of the different forms of racial violence and harassment and in particular gather more information on aspects of 'low-level' racial harassment.[1] The chapter begins by seeking to ascertain a measure of the different forms of racial violence and harassment and thereby get an overall estimate of the scale of the problem. People were asked whether they had been physically attacked; had had property damaged; or been verbally insulted or threatened for reasons to do with their 'race' or colour in the last twelve months. The number of times each type of incident occurred was then recorded. Respondents who had been victims of such racial violence and harassment were asked to describe each individual incident as fully as possible. For each incident, questions were asked about where it took place; who was responsible, including whether the perpetrator was known to the victim beforehand; and, whether the victim took any action to address the problem, particularly if they reported the incident to the police.

Research design

The findings reported from the qualitative research on racial violence and harassment formed part of a larger piece of research that comprised issues to do with ethnic identity, social care and health. The report on the research

Table 3   Details of interviews

Location	Caribbean Walthamstow Birmingham	Pakistani Walthamstow Birmingham	Bangladeshi Whitechapel Birminghan	Punjabi Gravesend Southall	Gujarati Leicester Southall
Depth interviews	15	8	8	8	8
Group discussions	10	5	2	5	5
First generation	10	4	4	4	4
Second generation	15	9	6	9	9
Men	10	8	5	6	6
Women	15	5	5	7	7
Total	25	13	10	13	13

undertaken on ethnic identity is reported in another volume (Modood et al 1994).

A total of 74 respondents participated in the research. The number of interviews that were carried out in each ethnic group was as follows.

25 with African Caribbeans
13 with Gujaratis
13 with Punjabis
13 with Pakistanis
10 with Bangladeshis

Of these 74 people, 35 were men and 39 were women. Twenty-six of the respondents were 'first generation' migrants defined as individuals who were born, received their schooling or worked until the age of 16 in their country of origin, and migrated to Britain as adults. Forty-eight of the respondents were members of the 'second generation' defined as individuals who were born in, or at least had received their schooling in Britain. Forty-seven of the 74 people were interviewed individually while the other 27 took part in group discussions.

Each of the minority ethnic groups were selected in the spring of 1993 in two locations where they formed a significant and settled population. This is an important point when it comes to studying racial violence and harassment because it is suspected there is much variation between areas and the two areas selected for each of the groups may not have been typical. The respondents were selected in a number of ways. The Punjabis and Gujaratis were selected by knocking on people's doors in the designated area and recruiting respondents until the desired number of each generation and gender was reached. The African Caribbean, Pakistani and Bangladeshi individual interviewees were selected through non-religious community organisations. Participants of the group discussions were found by a market research agency according to the two sift criteria laid down by the research team and by going to areas where it was known the communities resided.

First generation South Asians were offered the opportunity to be interviewed in their community languages. All 16 of them were interviewed in this way. Individuals were questioned through semi-structured interviews or through group discussion by an ethnically matched interviewer. The group discussions lasted an hour and a half whilst the individual interviews were between 45 and 60 minutes in length. Of this time, an average of ten minutes were taken up with questions to do with racial violence and harassment, although this clearly varied depending on the respondent's personal experience of the problem. The researcher in the group discussions took detailed notes during the course of the discussion as well as tape-recording the interview. In the individual interviews with the African Caribbeans, Pakistanis and Bangladeshis, the same procedure was adopted while for the Punjabis and Gujaratis detailed notes were undertaken during the course of the interview and written up afterwards.

The overall prevalence of racial violence and harassment

As shown by Table 4, about a third, that is 22, of the total of 74 respondents had suffered some form of racial violence or harassment in the past twelve months. The South Asians in the sample had a much higher rate of victimisation than African Caribbeans. Two-fifths that is 20, of the 49 South Asian respondents said they had experienced some form of racial violence or harassment in the past year compared to less than a tenth, that is two, of the 25 African Caribbean respondents. On the other hand, there was no significant difference in victimisation rates by gender.[2]

Each of the constituent parts of racial violence and harassment were then analysed in further detail by asking the victims about what insights they could provide about the location of such incidents and the type of person who engaged in such acts of racial violence and harassment, including whether the perpetrator was known to the victim beforehand. Finally, the victim was asked whether they took any action to address the problem, particularly if they reported the incident to the police.

Racial abuse and threatening behaviour

Table 4 shows that 18 of the 74 respondents had been racially abused or threatened in the past 12 months. It was found that almost all of the 22

Table 4 **The number of individuals who have been racially attacked or harassed in the last 12 months by ethnic group**

Ethnic group	Number of people in ethnic group	Overall number of people experiencing some form of racial violence or harassment	Number of people racially abused or threatened	Number of people racially attacked	Number of people whose property damaged due to their 'race'
Gujarati	13	3	3	1	1
Punjabi	13	9	7	3	0
Pakistani	13	3	2	1	1
Bangladeshi	10	5	5	2	2
African Caribbean	25	2	1	0	1
Total	74	22	18	7	5

respondents who said they had suffered some form of racial violence and harassment had experienced what is commonly known as its 'low-level' component.

The location of incidents of racial abuse and threatening behaviour
Table 5 shows that 18 respondents suffered a total of 24 incidents of racial abuse and threatening behaviour in the last 12 months. Some of the 18 respondents recounted multiple incidents of victimisation at different locations. However, the problem of repeat victimisation was not adequately addressed within this qualitative study. The records of the racially motivated incidents show that the respondents often reduced what was a series of several incidents of racial abuse and threatening behaviour to one single discrete incident. To illustrate the precise yet diverse nature of these types of incident, all of these accounts are recorded below.

Racial abuse at work and college
Seven of the total of 24 incidents of racial abuse and threatening behaviour took place at work. The perpetrators tended to be both customers and fellow workers.

One Gujarati man said he and other Gujaratis had been racially abused on several occasions by fellow white workers who objected to their speaking Gujarati together. The incidents had been reported to the supervisor and manager on a number of occasions but no action had been taken. As he

Table 5   The location of incidents of racial abuse and threatening behaviour

Location	Number of incidents of racial abuse and threatening behaviour
Place of work/ education	7
In or near the home	3
Public transport	2
Place of entertainment	3
In the street	9

n = 24

said, 'they just turned a blind eye to it all'. He continued that the situation facing Gujarati workers at his place of work was intolerable, particularly when management could have undertaken measures to address the problem.

A Punjabi woman shopkeeper was another victim of racial abuse at work, but this time on the telephone. This had occurred at least three times in the last three months. This woman felt particularly perturbed about these phone calls because they occurred only when her husband (who worked with her) was out. On occasions when her husband had picked up the phone the caller would stay on the line but would not speak which led her to suspect the caller was the same person making racist calls to her.

Another Punjabi woman who worked as a carer in an old people's home was racially abused by an elderly white patient. She said this patient had made comments such as 'don't touch me' and 'I don't like blacks' to her. This woman said she had little confidence in management taking action against this type of racial abuse and had consequently decided against reporting these incidents. Instead she had come to the conclusion that she would have to accept that incidents of racial abuse were 'all part and parcel of the job of caring'.

Similarly, an African Caribbean woman who worked as a home care officer said she was racially abused by a patient. Again, she had decided against reporting the perpetrator to management because she felt the racial abuse and threatening behaviour was an inevitable aspect of 'having to look after mentally ill patients'.

One incident of racial abuse occurred at school. The incident involved a female Bengali teacher who was racially abused by a fellow teacher in the staff room. She had been sitting with a number of other Bengali teachers showing pictures of a wedding she had recently attended and speaking in

Bengali when the offending teacher came in and said 'speaking bloody Bengali again, speak English'.

A Punjabi woman narrated how she had to experience racially insulting remarks from a white student in her class who 'told everyone in the class that her father had been on holiday and looked like one of them, pointing at me and other Asian students in the class..."a Paki"'.

A Pakistani man said that college was a location where incidents of racial abuse were commonplace. He explained how jokes about his 'race' and colour were a regular and integral part of his college life. He recounted numerous incidents where fellow white students had made racist jokes. Indeed, even some of his own white friends engaged in the telling of such jokes. Although he sometimes publicly objected, he felt it was very difficult to do so continually because you would then be considered 'a poor loser'.

Racial abuse in or near the home
Of the 24 incidents of racial abuse and threatening behaviour, three had occurred in the area where the victim lived.

One Gujarati woman and her family began to suffer racial harassment almost immediately they moved to a predominantly white residential area. The woman stated that 'we immediately became the gossip of the whole road... we've been stared at, got complaints from them over minor rebuilding work to the house and for playing music too loud'.

The white neighbours complained to the local council, asking them to investigate their complaints. This woman said she and her family had chosen to ignore this racial harassment rather than report it to anyone but acknowledged that it had caused them 'unwanted misery'.

A Bengali man recounted how he had been called 'Paki' and threatened by a white person who lived on the same road as him. He had initially decided to inform the police but had been dissuaded by a friend who said that he might suffer possible reprisals.

A Punjabi man also recounted an incident of racial harassment where he was spat at by a white youth who went to the same school and lived in the same road as himself.

Racial abuse on public transport
Of the 24 incidents of racial abuse and threatening behaviour, two had occurred on public transport. One Punjabi man recounted how he was spat at by a gang of white male youths when he was getting off a train at a mainline London station.

Similarly, another Punjabi man described how he had been racially abused by a group of white youths when waiting for a train.

Racial abuse at a place of entertainment

Of the 24 incidents of racial abuse and threatening behaviour, three had taken place at a place of entertainment. Two of the Punjabi women interviewed were racially abused by bouncers at a Central London nightclub who then proceeded to refuse them entry on the grounds that 'they were going to restrict the number of Asians coming into the club'. One of these Punjabi women was refused access to five Central London clubs in one night whilst out with some South Asian friends.

Finally, a Bengali man was racially abused, chased and threatened by a gang of white youths at a fair. He reported the incident to a policeman at the fair but the officer took no action.

Racial abuse in the street

Nine of the 24 incidents of racial abuse and threatening behaviour had occurred in the street. This was the most common location of incidents of 'low-level' racial harassment. All the incidents were similar in that the respondents had been racially abused or threatened by people unknown to them beforehand.

A Punjabi woman was called 'Paki' by a group of white youths when walking down the street while a Punjabi man was racially abused on the street by passing white youths in a car whilst walking with a South Asian friend. Similarly, one Pakistani man was called 'Paki' by passing white youths in a car. A Bengali woman was called 'Paki' by white schoolboys. A Bengali man was racially abused by a number of white people on the street. He said that he had been racially abused because he had a job and dressed well when going to work. These white people would often say 'look at that "Paki" taking our jobs'.

Four of the nine incidents of racial abuse and threatening behaviour in the street involved the police. These four cases were different from the other incidents of racial abuse and threatening behaviour recorded in this study in that the victims did not give any specific reason for thinking that racism was the motive for the police behaviour. However, after an analysis of these incidents it appears that the police behaviour in all these cases was at the very least unreasonable, and that racial antipathy almost certainly played a part in their harassing these particular people. Interestingly, the four incidents of police stops involved South Asians rather than African Caribbeans, which seems to go against the available evidence (see Smith and Gray 1985 and Shaw 1994).

The incidents included one where a Gujarati man in his car was stopped by the police and asked to open the boot. When they found hammers and chisels in a toolbox, they gave him a 'warning' for 'carrying offensive weapons' despite establishing that he was a carpenter by trade.

A Gujarati woman explained how she felt she had been racially harassed by the police when she was stopped and had her car searched for drugs. She outlined how the police treated her in a rude manner and continually questioned whether she was the owner of the vehicle. As she recalled, 'they searched my car for half an hour and kept asking me whose car it was'.

She also recounted several other incidents where 'on the way back from Central London, we get stopped all the time, especially if there are more than four Asians in the car. Every time we go to or are coming back from Central London this happens.'

Another Gujarati woman gave an example of where she had been stopped by the police who then questioned her competency to drive. She recounted several similar incidents that her friends had also experienced.

A Punjabi man recalled one incident where he was stopped by the police.

> I got stopped by the police for carrying a cricket bat. It was in a cover in a sports bag. The policeman came up to me and said, 'Excuse me son, can I have a look at your bat?' and began shaking it.

This youth perceived this incident as being part of the wider pattern of racial harassment of South Asian youth by the police who 'suspected they were up to no good'.

Perpetrators
Table 6 shows that almost all the people racially abused or threatened in or near their home or at work or study knew who the perpetrator was before the incident took place. On the other hand, none of the people who had been racially abused or threatened on public transport, in places of entertainment or in the street knew the identity of the perpetrators. In almost every incident of 'low level' racial harassment, the perpetrators were young white males.

Action taken
The victims were then asked what action they had taken when they were racially abused or threatened. Only one individual reported an incident of racial abuse or threatening behaviour to the police. A Bengali man had gone to the police and told them that he had been racially abused and threatened by a group of white youths at a fair. The police decided to take no action. In another incident, following complaints from teaching staff, the school authorities decided to dismiss a teacher who had made racially abusive remarks towards a fellow member of staff.

Table 6   The identification of perpetrators by location

Location	Number of incidents where the victim knew perpetrator
Work/ education	6 from 7
In or near the home	3 from 3
Public transport	0 from 2
Place of entertainment	0 from 3
In the street	0 from 9

n = 24 (18 respondents recounted a total of 24 incidents of racial abuse and threatening behaviour).

Racial attacks

The British Crime Survey states that '[South] Asians and African Caribbeans often reported that there was a racial element in violent incidents against them'. Thirty-seven per cent of all violent incidents against South Asians were felt to be racially motivated compared with 27 per cent of all violent incidents against African Caribbeans in the respondents' view. In addition, the relative incidence of racially motivated attacks on South Asians and African Caribbeans tended to differ to some extent by location.[3] South Asians reported a high incidence of racially motivated assaults in or around the home and in the street whereas African Caribbeans reported a high incidence of such types of assault at work and in clubs as well as in the street. Hence, for South Asians 64 per cent of all assaults in or around the home were felt to be racially motivated compared to 18 per cent of African Caribbeans. Both groups had a high incidence of racially motivated assaults in the street (53 per cent and 58 per cent respectively). However, 34 per cent of assaults at work and 24 per cent of assaults in clubs were thought to be racially motivated by African Caribbeans compared to 7 per cent and 5 per cent of South Asians in these locations (Aye Maung and Mirrlees-Black 1994: 15). Table 4 shows that seven of the 74 people interviewed in our own study said they had been physically attacked because of their 'race' or colour in the past year. All the seven people who had been racially attacked were South Asians.

Table 7   The location of incidents of racial attacks

Location	Number of incidents racially attack
Place of work/education	0
In or near the home	1
Public transport	1
Place of entertainment	0
In the street	5

n = 7 (None of the respondents recounted multiple incidents of physical attack in the past year)

The location of incidents of racial attacks

Table 7 shows that five of the seven racial attacks occurred in the street, one in or near the home and one on public transport.

A racial attack in or near the home

One person was physically attacked near where he lived. A Bengali man recounted how he was constantly harassed and racially abused on the estate where he lived in Wapping, east London. He felt it was because he was only the second non-white person on the estate and therefore isolated and an easy target for white racists. This man was not only verbally abused, but had bricks thrown through his windows and was constantly being 'kicked and punched'. However, he has since been moved off the estate and feels he is living in safer accommodation.

A racial attack on public transport

A Punjabi man explained how he was attacked by a group of white youths when he and some friends went to the aid of some young South Asians who were being racially abused and threatened in a bus garage. He recounted that the police were called but took no action against the white youths who continued to call him 'Paki' in their presence. Indeed, not only was there no action taken against the white youths by the police, one of the policeman actually began to racially insult him. And he continued 'when he was searching me, the policeman saw a chain around my neck with a picture of a Sikh God with a turban and beard and said "he needs a shave doesn't he?"'. In the end, the man said the police took no action against the white

35

...uths despite knowing 'it's a known skinhead haunt' and he felt they had been unsympathetic to him and his situation.

Racial attacks in the street

Five of the seven individuals were physically attacked in the street. A Gujarati man was beaten up by 'a gang of white boys' who called him 'Paki'. A Pakistani man was walking with a friend when he was physically attacked by three white boys with a brick. A Bengali woman was 'pushed and punched' by a group of white boys who called her 'Paki'. A Punjabi woman recounted how she and her mother were attacked in a subway by four white youths who then went on to steal all their belongings. In recounting the incident she highlighted graphically the nature of the attack:

> I was taking my mum to the clinic. I had a gold necklace on. Four white youths started following us... we knew they were following us but kept on walking. When we got to the subway, they jumped us... called us 'Pakis' and beat me and my mum up, stole everything and ran away.

Another Punjabi woman was attacked by a white man who also racially abused her while attempting to steal a gold necklace. She said that £50 worth of damage was caused to the necklace.

Perpetrators

On the whole, the people who carried out these racial attacks were again groups of young white males, including some of school age. The attackers were unknown to the victims in every instance apart from the case of the Bengali man who was racially harassed and attacked near his home.

Action taken

In only two of the seven cases of physical attack were the police contacted. The reasons for not reporting the incidents to the police are covered elsewhere in the report (see page 38). The two people who did contact the police about the physical attacks were both dissatisfied with the police response. As we saw earlier, the Punjabi youth who was physically attacked by a group of white youths at a bus garage, alleged that the police were not only unhelpful in dealing with the incident, but had also racially insulted him. In the second case, where the woman had a gold chain damaged, she said the police were 'not helpful at all'.

It is worth noting that the 1988 British Crime Survey found that satisfaction after reporting to the police was lower among ethnic minorities than among white people:

> 61 per cent of white victims said they were 'fairly' or 'very' satisfied with the way the police dealt with the matter, as against 49 per cent of Afro-Caribbeans

and 44 per cent of [South] Asian victims. Both Afro-Caribbean and [South] Asian victims were more likely than whites to feel that the police did not do enough. Afro-Caribbean victims more often perceived impoliteness or unpleasantness on the part of the police, and they were more likely to feel that the police should have apprehended the offender. [South] Asian victims were relatively more dissatisfied because the police did not appear interested. (Mayhew, Elliot and Dowds 1989: 28-29)

Racially motivated damage to property
Table 4 showed that five of the 74 people said they had had their property damaged in the past year for reasons to do with their race or colour. In four of the five incidents, the victims were South Asians.

Damage to the house
A Pakistani man was a victim of continual racial harassment over a period of five years from different white, male youths who in the most extreme case had thrown stones and broken the windows of his house.

A Bengali woman had the windows of her house smashed and a fire started on her front doormat by a group of white youths.

We have already heard the case of a Bengali man who was continually harassed, racially abused and attacked, being one of only two non-white people living on the estate. This man had also had his windows broken by white youths throwing bricks.

Damage to the car
A Gujarati man said he had his car broken into on several occasions in the past year. He strongly suspected at least some of these incidents were racially motivated because several white people who lived near him had often remarked about him and other South Asians as being '"show-offs"... They think their white friends are forced to break into cars because of poverty and unemployment.'

An African Caribbean woman had a brick thrown at her car window by a white man shouting racial abuse.

Perpetrators
The victims of racially motivated damage to property were asked to describe the people who had undertaken these acts and whether they knew them beforehand. In all three of the incidents where the house had been damaged, the victims identified the perpetrators as being young, white males who lived in the same residential area. In the two incidents where the victim's car was damaged the perpetrator was unknown.

37

Action taken

Three of the five incidents where the property of the victim was damaged as a result of a racial motive were reported to the police. However, in all these cases, the victims were dissatisfied with the action taken. The individual who had his car damaged on several occasions felt 'the police were of no use' and he had little confidence in them dealing with the matter effectively. Similarly, the person who had been racially harassed consistently for the past five years argued he had reported many of these incidents to the police and had even sought to resolve the problem through political channels via his local Labour Party but 'to no avail'. He felt his situation to be beyond hope and said 'no-one could help'.

The response of the police to the third incident which was reported to them was particularly disturbing. An African Caribbean woman who had a brick thrown breaking her car window while also being racially abused by a white man was told by the investigating police officer that he was not going to take any action against the perpetrator because the brick had not hit her and he was coming to the end of his shift and did not wish to do any further paperwork. The police officer dismissed the woman's request to take action against the man for racially abusing her as being the equivalent of calling someone overweight. He told her that if she wished to pursue the incident further, she would have to contact the perpetrator herself.

Consequently, the African Caribbean woman brought her brother along with a tape recorder to get the man to admit on tape what he had done. However, the white man, although admitting to the incident, proceeded to throw another brick, breaking the brother's car window. The brother responded by throwing the brick through the window of the white man's house. At this, the white man went into the house and came out with a knife and threatened the brother. By this time the police had been called again; they arrested the brother of the African Caribbean woman but took no action against the white man. Although in the end no charges were made against either party, this incident was particularly worrying because the failure of the police officers to address the initial complaint led directly to an escalation of the problem and a further offence being committed.

The non-reporting of incidents of racial violence and harassment to the police

Those people who had suffered any form of racial violence and harassment but had not reported it to the police were asked to explain the reasons for their decision. Broadly speaking, the study found that respondents did not report incidents of racial harassment to the police for three reasons.

- Having to live, work and learn beside the people who racially harassed them meant there was a danger of reprisals and further harassment if the incidents were reported. Hence, many felt they would only worsen the situation by reporting the perpetrators to the police.

- People did not believe that incidents of racial harassment would be dealt with effectively by the police. This view was reinforced for some by their own personal experiences with the police where incidents of racial harassment had not been investigated thoroughly. Some respondents also felt the police were unlikely to treat those incidents of 'low-level' racial harassment seriously because they refused to recognise a pattern of repeat victimisation and instead tended to treat such incidents in isolation thereby 'trivialising them'.

- The police were regarded by some of the people interviewed as being 'part of the problem' of racial violence and harassment rather than an organisation capable of dealing with it effectively.

Summary
This chapter has sought to explore the nature of each of the constituent parts of racial violence and harassment. Attention has been particularly paid to the wide range of incidents that constitute what is referred to as 'low level' racial harassment. The study found that about a third of all respondents had suffered some form of racial violence and harassment in the past year. South Asians were more likely to have been victims of racial violence and harassment than African Caribbeans.

A quarter of all respondents said they had been racially abused or threatened in the last twelve months. These incidents of racial abuse and threatening behaviour occurred in a wide variety of locations that included the victim's place of work or study; in or near the home; places of entertainment; while using public transport and in the street. Whether the victims were likely to have known the perpetrators beforehand was dependent on the location. Almost every person who had been racially abused or threatened in their place of work or study or in or near the home knew the perpetrator beforehand whereas none of those who had been racially abused or threatened in the street, on public transport or in a place of entertainment did so. Four of the victims reported they had been racially insulted or threatened by police officers. The type of person who engaged in this 'low level' racial harassment tended to be almost always a young white male, acting as part of a group.

These incidents were rarely reported to any official body. Only two of the 24 incidents of racial abuse were reported by the victims. The one person who reported it to the police was disappointed by their response. On the other hand, racial abuse directed at a Bengali teacher by a fellow member of the teaching staff did result in the dismissal of the offender by the school authorities.

About one in ten people reported they had been racially attacked in the past year. Most of these racial attacks constituted common assaults rather than serious woundings. On the whole, racial attacks tended to occur in the street and were carried out by groups of young white males. Two of the seven cases of racial attack were reported to the police. Both the victims revealed their dissatisfaction with the response of the police in addressing the problem.

Five of the 74 respondents reported that they had been victims of racially motivated damage to property. In most of these cases, this had involved the breaking of windows of the victim's house or car. However, in one case, a fire was started on the front doormat of a woman's house. In the three cases of racially motivated damage to the house, the victim identified the perpetrators as being young white males who lived in the same residential areas. Three of the five cases were reported to the police, but the victim tended to be disappointed with the response of the police. Indeed in one case, not only did the police officer fail to address the initial complaint, but their refusal to do so led directly to an escalation of the problem and another offence being committed.

Notes

1. It needs to be reiterated that 'low-level' racial harassment is difficult to capture in quantitative research because of the wide range of incidents that it can encompass. A number of local studies have made an attempt to capture this form of racial violence and harassment by asking questions about a specific type of incident that is considered to be indicative of this form of racial harassment (see Walsh 1987). As a result, it is contended that you can get at least a reasonable estimate of the extent of the problem of 'low-level' racial harassment. However, it is extremely difficult to find an incident which is indicative of all the types of incident that can potentially fall into this category. As a result, you are likely to get only a partial picture of the extent of this form of racial harassment. There is no doubt that it is problematic to find a wording which manages to encompass the various types of incident without asking questions on each type of incident. Therefore, a question that seeks to tap into this form of racial harassment effectively must be sufficiently comprehensive to capture incidents as wide-ranging as verbal abuse, malicious complaints, spitting, graffiti, telephone harassment, racist mail and other types of nuisance behaviour. It is believed that the present study, by asking a question which sought to be wide-ranging in its scope, has attained this and thereby gathered a relatively comprehensive picture of the nature of this form of racial harassment.

2. Although statistical tests were carried out in this study, the conclusions based on these should be treated with caution because of the non-representative nature of the sample.

3. The British Crime Survey notes that this may be because 'Afro-Caribbeans work and socialise more in mixed ethnic settings' (Mayhew, Aye Maung and Mirrlees-Black 1993: 87).

4 The effect of racial harassment on people's lifestyle

Introduction

Little is known about what Gordon (1989) has called the 'hidden injuries of racism', that is, how the lives of South Asian and African Caribbean people are affected beyond the actual harassment that takes place. The Home Affairs Committee (1989: viii) recognised it was an aspect of the problem that required attention when it recommended that

> One priority should be to develop ways to reduce fear among ethnic minorities since the fear of racially motivated incidents, just as much as racial attacks and harassment themselves, casts a blight on the lives of members of ethnic minority communities in the UK.

The 1992 BCS asked whether respondents thought that racially motivated attacks were a problem in their area. Overall, it found few respondents who thought that racially motivated attacks were either a 'very' or 'fairly big' problem. Both African Caribbeans and South Asians were more likely than whites to think that they were a problem in their area. In particular, 18 per cent of South Asians and 12 per cent of African Caribbeans living in inner city areas thought that racially motivated attacks were a 'very' or 'fairly big' problem compared to 5 per cent of whites living in these areas. On the other hand, 10 per cent of both African Caribbeans and South Asians living outside the inner city areas thought that racially motivated attacks were a 'very' or 'fairly big' problem compared to 2 per cent of whites living in such areas (Aye Maung and Mirrlees-Black 1994: 11).

It is also worth looking at the 1992 British Crime Survey findings in relation to the fear of crime. The term 'fear of crime' is widely used as a convenient shorthand for emotional reactions ranging from mild concern to pervasive anxiety that result from awareness of the risk of experiencing crime (Mirrlees-Black and Aye Maung 1994: 2). The authors note that measuring the fear of crime is a subject of much debate. The 1992 BCS attempted to measure this 'fear of crime' by asking respondents how worried they were about falling victim to specific crimes. In addition, they were also asked about how safe they felt out alone at night and at home at night. People tended to be more concerned about being out alone at night than being at home alone at night. Overall, 32 per cent said they would feel 'very' or 'fairly' unsafe when walking out alone at night compared to 11 per cent who said they felt 'very' or 'fairly' unsafe when at home alone at night. The 1992 BCS also found that 'Asians and Afro-Caribbeans were more fearful than white respondents of being out alone after dark' (Mirrlees-Black and Aye Maung 1994: 2-4).

Adapting the way you lead your life because of the fear of being racially harassed

People in our study were asked whether they were constrained or had changed the way they lead their life because of the fear of being racially harassed, and then to describe fully the various ways in which they were.

Table 8 shows that one third, that is 24 of a total of 74 respondents felt that they were constrained in the way they led their life because of the fear of being racially harassed. The study also found a link between those people who had experienced some form of racial violence or harassment in the last 12 months and those who said the fear of racial harassment had affected the way they led their life. More than half, that is, 13 of the 22 individuals who had experienced some form of racial violence or harassment in the past year also said the fear of racial harassment had affected the way they led their life. Less than a quarter, that is, 11 of the 52 individuals who had not experienced any form of racial harassment in the past year said this. This seems to confirm the finding from the 1992 BCS that 'having been the

Table 8   **The number of people who were constrained in the way they led their life because of the fear of being racially harassed (by ethnic group)**

Ethnic group	Racial harassment affected lifestyle
Gujarati	7 out of 13
Punjabi	10 out of 13
Pakistani	1 out of 13
Bangladeshi	4 out of 10
African Caribbean	2 out of 25

n = 74

victim of crime oneself in the past is highly related to most of the fear measures' (Mirrlees-Black and Aye Maung 1994: 4).

Those respondents who said there life was constrained by the fear of being racially harassed were then asked to describe fully the ways in which this manifested itself.

Table 9   The ways in which people's lives were constrained by the fear of being racially harassed

The ways in which people's lives were constrained	The number of people whose lives were constrained by the fear of being racially harassed
Choosing a place to live	6
Constraints on going:	
- out at night near home	7
- to mainly white areas	8
- to places of entertainment	9
- on public transport	2
- to area of work/education	1

n = 24 (a number of individuals gave multiple answers)

Choosing a place to live
Six respondents said that the fear of being racially harassed had been a factor in determining the area in which they had decided to live. These six people, who were all South Asians, said it was important for them to live in an area with a high concentration of South Asians in order for them to feel safe. Some were fearful of being physically attacked or harassed if they went outside their 'own Asian area'. One woman explained how she became a victim of racial harassment almost immediately she moved from an ethnically-mixed area to one that was predominantly white. As she said: 'As soon as I go out of an Asian area, I'm faced with racism'.

On the other hand, some South Asian women explained that the fear of being racially harassed was compounded by the fear of being sexually harassed by some men of all ethnic groups. Consequently, they argued that they would feel just as unsafe living in areas with high concentrations of South Asians as in predominantly white residential areas.

Going out at night near home
One of the most important constraints imposed by the fear of being racially harassed was on going out at night, including in the area where the person lived. Seven people said they would not even consider going out at night for fear of being racially harassed and several said they felt 'like prisoners in their own home'. As one Gujarati woman explained:

> This [the fear of racial harassment] has affected the way I live my life tremendously. We are not free to go anywhere, especially at night. You would always be afraid of being injured, having your car damaged or your family hurt.

Going to predominantly white residential areas
Eight respondents said they avoided going out to predominantly white residential areas for fear of being racially harassed. One Punjabi woman said she avoided such areas because she would be stopped and harassed by the police who would 'suspect she was up to mischief' because South Asians were not expected to be in the area.

Going out to places of entertainment
Nine individuals explained how they were reluctant to go to particular places of entertainment for fear of being racially harassed. Many of them said their socialising patterns were regularly constrained by the need to avoid venues where there would be large concentrations of white people present. All nine people cited the pub as a place they would feel uneasy about going to because of their fear of being racially harassed. One man explained how he avoided going to pubs in central London at weekends because he felt uncomfortable when waiting to meet friends since white people stared at him 'when I walk in, trying to work out if I am foreigner or not'. Similarly, a woman explained how she was made to feel uncomfortable in a pub because of the way white 'people are watching me. I am aware of my colour.' Several individuals mentioned that they avoided social arenas such as the cinema, nightclubs, restaurants and leisure centres, particularly at weekends. Finally, two individuals mentioned they would never go to football matches because of the fear of racial violence and harassment.

Going on public transport
Two women said they avoided travelling on the tubes and railways alone, particularly at night, because of their worry about being racially harassed.

Going to the area of work or place of study

One woman expressed her concern about being racially harassed in the area where she went to study. She explained how she often had to drive two miles away from the area to eat lunch and always made sure she left the college premises before it got dark. As she said:

> You're weary of it [the fear of racial harassment] 24 hours a day. It's not a case of being able to change the way you look. You get up and look in the mirror and you're aware of it... in London, I do feel as though people are watching you all the time.

Minority ethnic response to the fear of racial harassment

Despite the obvious importance of establishing the scale and nature of racial violence and harassment facing minority ethnic people, it is equally important to recount how these people have actually sought to tackle and resist it. We saw in the introduction how people have established local anti-racist groups, including self defence groups in some areas to protect themselves from racial violence. In addition, they have continued to demand a more effective response in tackling the problem from official organisations such as the police and local councils.

It has just been outlined how many individuals have been forced to adapt the way they lead their life because of the fear of being racially harassed. On the other hand, several others in the study sought to address the problem in other ways. A number of individuals said they refused to let the fear of racial violence and harassment affect the way they lead their lives as adults. They argued that when they had been children, the fear of being racially harassed had forced them to lead very restricted lives with their parents preventing them from going outside their homes to play or engaging in any social activities. They felt strongly that they would not allow this to happen with their own children and that members of minority ethnic groups should actively tackle the racism that they faced. Three other individuals also said they would not let the fear of racial violence and harassment affect how they led their lives. One woman explained how this fear had been an important factor in many of her friends' decisions to choose which university they attended. However, she refused to take this into account:

> I haven't really taken it as a factor because I don't feel I should have to choose where I want to study because of the colour I am. But I have got loads of friends who are at Birmingham, Leicester, Sheffield, because they know they will be safe with other Asians there.

Summary

Little is known about how the lives of South Asians and African Caribbean people are affected beyond the actual harassment they experience. The qualitative study revealed that about a third of all people said they were constrained in the way they led their life because of fear of being racially harassed. The fear of being racially harassed affected the quality of life that many of these people could live. It was an important factor for some in deciding where to live. It placed a number of restrictions on their social lives with some not prepared to go out at night even in or near the area they lived; while others were concerned about going out in areas where mostly white people lived; and some were not prepared to use public transport. However, it is important to emphasise that minority ethnic communities are not just passive victims of racial violence and harassment. Rather, it is a problem they tackle and actively resist. Several individuals in the qualitative study explained how they refused to let the fear of being racially harassed affect the way they lead their life as young adults in Britain.

5 Summary and conclusions

Summary of findings

A number of recent developments have served to focus attention on the problem of racial violence and harassment in Britain. Of most concern has been the volume and alarming nature of physical attacks in parts of east London. Although it is not always clear how far actions on the street relate to developments in the political sphere, rising violence has been accompanied by the electoral emergence of the far-right BNP who have established a presence within several local wards in the east London Boroughs of Tower Hamlets and Newham.

These developments in Britain have been reflected in disturbing racial violence in parts of Europe, and the electoral success of far-right parties. In Italy, the fascist National Alliance recently formed part of the government. In France, The Front Nationale has established a strong presence in national elections and is well represented in the European Parliament. On the other hand, the electoral success of the German far-right Republikaner Party has waned recently but concern remains about the continuing level of racial violence.

However, the minority ethnic communities have not been passive victims of racial violence and harassment in Britain. In addition to calling for local councils and the police to address the problem more effectively they have established local groups which provide advice and support to people who have been racially attacked or harassed. Similarly, the apprehension that events in east London may be the precursor to racial violence and harassment in other parts of the country have led to the establishment of two national anti-racist organisations – the Anti-Nazi League (ANL) and the Anti-Racist Alliance (ARA).

There has been concern in official circles too. The Home Office and the Department of the Environment have both developed policies on racial violence and harassment. The House of Commons Select Committee published a report on racial attacks and harassment in 1994, with a number of recommendations for tackling the problem more effectively.

A first step towards a better understanding of the phenomenon is to establish the nature and scale of the problem. This has been greatly contested because of the lack of national data available on the problem. However, since 1988, there have been two national data sets which provide information on levels of racial violence and harassment in Britain.

The first of these, statistics on incidents reported to the police, suggested there were nearly 10,000 racially motivated incidents in 1993/94, a 120 per cent increase since 1988. However, this finding needs to be treated with caution. The victims of racially motivated incidents do not necessarily report them to the police. The increase in recorded levels of the problem could potentially represent changes in the behaviour of any of the three parties: more racially motivated incidents undertaken by the perpetrators; more of those crimes reported by the victims; or more of those reports recorded as racially motivated incidents by the police.

The second data set which provides information on levels of racial violence and harassment is the British Crime Survey (BCS). By covering people's experience of racially motivated crime irrespective of whether it has been reported to the police, this victimisation survey gives a more accurate picture of the scale of the problem. The survey estimated there had been a total of 130,000 racially motivated crimes against South Asians and African Caribbeans in 1991, comprising 89,000 against South Asians and 41,000 against African Caribbeans. This greatly exceeds the estimates based on police statistics. The BCS indicated only a slight increase in the number of racially motivated crimes between 1987 and 1991, though there was an increase in the rate of reporting to the police.

The British Crime Survey therefore suggests that although the level of racial violence and harassment has been steadier than the police statistics indicated, the overall number of incidents throughout the period has been far higher than people had realised.

Although this victimisation survey represented a step forward in providing a more accurate estimate than had been provided by the police statistics, it remains only a partial picture. The BCS asks questions about selected kinds of criminal activity, and then asks minority ethnic victims whether they thought each incident was racially motivated. Although there was a specific question about whether threats were racially motivated, the questionnaire failed to cover a range of non-criminal incidents such as racial abuse, malicious complaints, and other types of insulting behaviour which have been referred to as 'low-level' racial harassment. 'Low level' racial harassment has been an aspect of the problem that has been greatly neglected when attempting to understand the nature of the phenomenon. These types of incident, although not criminal, can represent an equally serious form of the problem, especially if they are part of a campaign of harassment.

It is of increasing importance, particularly in the light of recent developments in both Britain and Europe, to have a regular national survey on racial violence and harassment which is able to provide an overall picture of the scale of the problem in Britain and which allows changes over time to be regularly measured. The Home Affairs Select Committee (1994: Vol.2 pp.x) 'strongly recommend[ed] that the Government improves its performance in providing statistics to judge the nature and extent of racial attacks and harassment' and repeated its recommendation, first made in its report of 1989, for the government to commission a national survey to examine the occurrence of racial attacks and harassment nationally. A detailed survey would not simply count the number of racially motivated incidents but also distinguish between the different forms that it can take. Furthermore, such a national survey could be used to identify those areas where the problem is most prevalent to enable more detailed follow-up work to be undertaken in order to explain local variations in the incidence of the problem in terms of the composition of the population, and the series of social, economic and historical factors which might influence the scale of the problem. A much more subtle understanding of the phenomenon is needed before a more effective policy response can be developed.

Our qualitative interviews sought to explore the nature of the various constituent parts of racial violence and harassment, with particular attention being paid to the wide range of incidents that constitute 'low level' racial harassment. The study found that about a third of all respondents had suffered some form of racial violence and harassment in the past year. The South Asians were more likely to have been victims of racial violence and harassment than African Caribbeans, though we are not sure that this finding would be replicated in a representative national sample.

Three types of violence and harassment were identified among the 74 respondents:

- racial abuse or threatening behaviour (24 incidents);
- physical attacks (7 incidents);
- damage to property (5 incidents).

The incidents of racial abuse and threatening behaviour occurred in a wide variety of locations that included the victim's place of work or study; in or near the home; places of entertainment; while using public transport; and in the street.

Almost all those who had been racially abused or threatened in their place of work or study, or in or near the home, knew the perpetrator beforehand whereas none of those who had been racially abused or threatened in the street, on public transport or in a place of entertainment knew the perpetrator beforehand. Four of the victims reported they had been racially insulted or threatened by police officers. The type of person engaged in this form of racial harassment tended to be almost always a young white male (usually in a group).

On the whole, these incidents were not reported to any official organisation. Only two of the 24 incidents of racial abuse and threatening behaviour were reported by the victims. The person who reported being racially abused and threatened to the police was disappointed by their failure to tackle the problem seriously. On the other hand, racial abuse directed at a Bengali teacher by a fellow member of the teaching staff did result in the dismissal of the offender.

About one in ten people reported they had been racially attacked in the past year. Most of these racial attacks constituted common assaults rather than serious woundings. On the whole, racial attacks tended to occur in the street and were carried out by groups of young white males, sometimes of school age. Two of the seven cases of racial attack were reported to the police. Both the victims revealed their dissatisfaction with the response of the police in addressing the problem.

Five of the 74 respondents reported that they had been victims of racially motivated damage to property. Most cases had involved the breaking of windows of the victim's house or car. However, in one case, a fire was started on the front doormat of a woman's house. In the three cases of racially motivated damage to the house, the victim again identified the perpetrators as being young white males who lived in the same residential areas. Three of the five cases were reported to the police, but these victims tended also to be disappointed with the response of the police. Indeed in one case, not only did the police officer fail to address the initial complaint, but their refusal to do so led directly to an escalation of the problem and another offence being committed.

Little is also known about the 'hidden injuries of racism', that is, how the lives of South Asians and African Caribbean people are affected beyond the actual harassment that takes place. About a third of the people interviewed said the way they led their life was constrained in some way by the fear of being racially harassed. Those people who had experienced some form of racial violence and harassment in the last 12 months were especially likely to say that the fear of racial harassment had affected the way they led their life.

The fear of being racially harassed was an important factor for some in deciding where to live. It placed a number of constraints on their social lives with some people not prepared to go out at night, even locally; others expressed concern about going out in areas where mostly white people lived; others were not prepared to use public transport.

Policy implications

Herman Ouseley, the first black chair of the Commission for Racial Equality (CRE) said recently that the CRE has

> identified a society free from racial prejudice and attacks as being a pre-requisite for a just society based on racial equality and free from racial discrimination. (Foreword by Herman Ouseley in Seager, R. and Jeffrey, J. (1994))

The more we learn about racial violence and harassment, the clearer it becomes that the publicly reported police statistics represent the visible tip of the iceberg. The 10,000 reported incidents no doubt include the majority of the most serious and violent cases. However, the British Crime Survey revealed more than ten times that number of criminal events which appeared to the victims to have been racially motivated. Our own interviews suggest that there are other, and potentially much larger, forms of racially insulting and threatening behaviour which are not seen as criminal events in themselves. This pyramid of violence and harassment must be based on a continuing level of racial prejudice and antagonism in sections of the white population of which harassment is only a sympton.

It is important to form a judgement about the relationship between these types of racial violence and harassment. It would be counter-productive to suggest that every time research digs deeper to reveal ten or a hundred times as many incidents as had previously been known about, that meant the problem was ten or a hundred times as serious. As an individual event, an epithet shouted across a road is trivial compared to grievous bodily harm, or even murder. It only cheapens our revulsion at the latter to pretend otherwise.

But it would be just as wrong to understate the importance of the 'low level' form of harassment. In the first place, the incidents should not be seen just as individual events. When they are linked together as a series, they create a continued climate of insecurity amongst the victims. As the former minister of state at the Home Office Peter Lloyd said, people

> should be concerned about smaller incidents and harassment. Although each incident is not very significant, with repetition they become corrosive, deeply hurtful and destructive. (*Hansard,* 10 February 1994)

Second, the widespread experience of 'low-level' harassment shows that overt racial hostility is not confined to a handful of white people, affecting only a few members of the minority ethnic groups. The really serious cases are not just isolated incidents – they are part of a pattern of hostility in which a large number of white youths resent and confront the minority community as a whole.

Third, attempts to downgrade the importance of 'low-level' harassment risk dismissing the specifically racist element. All civilised people are horrified by racially motivated attacks and murders, partly because they disapprove of all attacks and murders. When a black or Asian person is taunted about his or her colour, that is pure racism, unaffected by any other considerations.

Fourth, the serious and violent incidents should be seen as extreme examples of an underlying climate of racism that exists in Britain today. The underlying level of harassment is serious not only in its own right, but also as the breeding ground for violence.

These considerations point to the need to develop an approach to racial violence and harassment which encompasses all the different types of the problem. But it will immediately be apparent that the traditional discussion of harassment as a crime to be dealt with by the law, the police and the courts does not deal adequately with the range of issues raised by 'low-level' harassment. Consideration of the content and enforcement of law should certainly be included in a policy, but we will argue below for a much broader ranging approach to the problem.

The law on racial harassment

A number of organisations, ranging from the all party Home Affairs Select Committee on racial attacks and harassment (1994), the Labour Party, the Commission for Racial Equality (CRE) to campaigning organisations like the Anti-Racist Alliance (ARA) have called for a new offence of racial violence to be created. More recently, Paul Condon, Metropolitan Police Commissioner, has also welcomed such calls for a new law saying it would be a 'help rather than a hindrance' (cited in the *Voice* 12 July 1994).

It is contended that the creation of a specific offence of racial violence would serve three purposes. Firstly, it would demonstrate unambiguously the government's and society's abhorrence of this kind of crime. Secondly, it would enhance the confidence of ethnic minorities in the criminal justice system. Thirdly, it would allow the judiciary to deal more effectively with racially motivated crime. The Home Affairs Select Committee (1994) on racial attacks and harassment put forward the recommendation that whenever there is a charge of violent assault and there is sufficient evidence that the violence was racially motivated, a separate charge should be added to the indictment. If the jury then decided the person was guilty of the offence and that it was racially motivated, an additional and consecutive sentence should be imposed on the offender of up to five years imprisonment for the racial element in that offence.

Others have contended that such a law should also take account of how religious bigotry can be intertwined with violent racism arguing that otherwise anti-Muslim harassment and violence would slip through the net in the way that anti-Muslim discrimination does in respect of the 1976 Race Relations Act (Modood 1994: 15).

However, there has been opposition to the creation of a new offence of racially motivated violence from both the government and several anti-racist groups. The central criticism of anti-racist groups like the Campaign Against Racism and Fascism (CARF) is that legislation already exists to deal effectively with the problem and that what is required is a greater will to enforce these remedies. Bridges (1993: 69) has argued that

> there has been a failure of political will at all levels – among national and local
> leaders, local authority officialdom, the police and prosecuting authorities, and
> the courts – actively and effectively to bring the wide range of existing laws
> to bear on those carrying out racial attacks and harassment.

Critics of a new offence of racial violence have also argued that 'race relations' may worsen if racial violence were singled out as a crime requiring special legal treatment. It is argued that this would allow racists to claim they are the victims of special 'race' laws.

There is already specific provision for racially motivated criminal acts in the Public Order Act 1986 which states:

- a person is guilty of an offence where he or she uses threatening abusive or insulting words or behaviour, or displays any written material which is threatening, abusive or insulting if it is intended to stir up racial hatred;

- a person is guilty of an offence where he or she publishes such material;

- possessing racially inflammatory material is an offence.

A person convicted under these provisions is liable to imprisonment for up to two years. But the racial hatred provisions within this legislation have rarely been used. The number of prosecutions for publishing racially-inciting material rose from four in 1986 to 65 in 1991 (Labour Research February 1994: 8).

The debate about new legislation needs to take account of the different forms of the problem. The existing law offers severe penalties for such crimes as assault, and the courts are allowed to take account of the assailant's motives in determining a sentence. Would the primary object of a new law and of longer prison terms be to express society's disapproval of the crime, or to deter potential criminals? It is to be doubted whether a young male looking to attack a black or Asian person would be deterred by the risk of a double term in prison if a racial motive was established, where he was not already influenced by the probability of a long stretch under existing legislation.

It is at the other end of the scale that changes in the law might be more appropriate. There are some existing provisions which can be brought to bear. These include the 1988 Malicious Communications Act when the victim has been the recipient of 'poison pen letters'; the 1984 Telecom Act to deal with abusive telephone calls; and the Environmental Protection Act 1990 to deal with noise nuisance campaigns. But the police and the courts might be able to deal more directly with low level harassment if a new law made it an offence to taunt or abuse a member of another ethnic or religious group, where no other crime was being committed.

No laws and penalties will be of much use in dealing with isolated minor incidents. But legislation forbidding 'taunt or abuse' might be particularly valuable in dealing with repeat victimisation. Some individuals and families can be victims of continuous racial violence and harassment, often by the same group of people. It is difficult for the police to prosecute on the basis of each episode, but a charge based on a series of incidents could prove effective. Bridges (1994) has called for legislation which would allow for a conviction if two or more crimes have been committed against a person, his or her immediate family or property, with evidence that the perpetrator (of whatever 'race') acted in part on the basis of the victim's racial identity.

The role of the police

Part of the debate about legislation is concerned about the role of the police. Do they take adequate action in response to reports of racially motivated incidents?

Evidence from the BCS shows that the police campaign to encourage victims of racial violence and harassment to come forward has been partially successful. Nevertheless, well over half of all victims of racially motivated incidents still do not report them to the police. Our own qualitative study showed there is still a lack of confidence about whether the police treat reported incidents of racial violence and harassment seriously. Many victims had not reported their experiences. Among those who had, most expressed disappointment at the result: the victims often felt that the police had treated harassment as a trivial incident, and had not taken appropriate action.

There are two possible reasons why the police might respond ineffectually to complaints of 'low-level' racial violence and harassment. One might be that there is not much that they can do, in practice. Millions of reported crimes are effectively ignored every year because the effort of investigating, obtaining proof and prosecuting would be disproportionate to the severity of the crime and the probability of obtaining a conviction. This might be true of 'low-level' harassment just as it is of theft of bicycles. But if that is the police's policy, it is open to public debate; and if Parliament thinks harassment should be investigated more rigorously than bicycle theft, it should say so by increasing the scale of the penalties available.

In practice, though, it is individual police officers who make judgements about whether a complaint is worth following up. The attitude of the police themselves is therefore an important consideration. The higher echelons of the police force such as the Association of Chief Police Officers (ACPO) do take the issue of racial violence and harassment seriously. But concern remains about whether the frontline police culture has been affected by the ACPO stance. The qualitative study highlighted several examples where police officers themselves were perceived as being the perpetrators of racial harassment – 'part of the problem', rather than an organisation to which victims should turn for help.

It is clear, therefore, that senior officers need to continue their three-pronged strategy: encouraging victims of racial violence and harassment to come forward; emphasising to their frontline staff the need to recognise, record and investigate the incidents reported to them; and making it clear that harassment by police officers themselves will not be tolerated.

Much of the discussion of the role of the police is concerned with their decisions on whether or not to investigate and prosecute after the event. Another set of issues concerns their potential activities as keepers of the peace, preventing racial violence and harassment rather than punishing it. How often and how visibly do they patrol areas of known tension? How fast do they respond to calls for help, and how vigorously? Some minority families have been subjected to sustained campaigns of intimidation which would not have been allowed to continue if the victim had lived in Downing Street. How serious does the problem have to be before the police make a real and effective commitment to protecting those people who are subject to such racial violence and harassment?

A broader policy

Liberal and left-of-centre commentators are generally critical of the government's heavy-handed and punitive stance on general law and order issues. The causes of crime need to be understood, and prison is more concerned with meeting society's need to inflict punishment than with reforming criminals or deterring potential criminals. But when it comes to racial violence, these reservations are put aside, and calls are made for more vigorous prosecutions and heavier sentences.

There is no doubt that more appropriate laws and effective enforcement are necessary components of a policy to reduce and eliminate racial violence and harassment. But these tools cannot solve the problems on their own, any more than they have eliminated the wave of other types of crime committed. The underlying problem lies in how different groups of people interact with each other in their local communities; this is not an aspect of human life that can be controlled (though it may be influenced) by the law.

- More research, of the type started in this study, will help to identify the various situations where minority ethnic groups are at risk. There is then a whole range of organisations which can influence the extent to which racial violence and harassment is accepted or rejected from day to day.

- Many of the complaints concerned harassment at work. Employers could take a much stronger initiative than they do at present in helping to create a workplace culture which makes it clear to their staff, and even to customers, that racial harassment will not be tolerated. Employers should consider making racial violence and harassment an offence within their disciplinary codes and policies to enable the perpetrators to be brought to book under the normal disciplinary machinery.

- Much harassment occurs in and around the victim's homes. Local authorities have an important role to play, both as landlords and as town planners, in identifying trouble spots, allocating accommodation, reprimanding tenants for racist activities and so on.

- Other incidents occur in public places such as the street, buses and trains, places of entertainment and so on. These areas are partly the responsibility of the police, but also of shopkeepers, bus conductors, and others. They may not be responsible for racial harassment; but they could be encouraged to make themselves responsible for preventing it.

Looking wider still, there are many organisations which influence public opinion in one way or another – schools, the media, advertisers and so on. Each of them could play some positive role in the campaign against racial intolerance if they decided that the issue was important enough.

The campaign will not be effective, though, until research has provided a clearer understanding of the motives of those who perpetrate racial violence and harassment. It is not clear whether the harassers are an isolated minority of young men, alienated by 'failure' at school and in the labour market, and anxious to vent anger on a rival group perceived to have overtaken them in the social hierarchy, or whether their actions are an aggressive expression of racial prejudice which spreads much wider in the communities of which they are members.

It is a matter of urgency that effective action be taken by both official agencies and ordinary citizens if the problem of racial violence and harassment is to be prevented from becoming a worse national affliction.

References

Anti-Racist Alliance (1993) *Outlaw racial harassment* (London: Central Race Equality Unit, London Borough of Greenwich)

Aye Maung, N. and Mirrlees-Black, C. (1994) *Racially motivated crime: a British Crime Survey analysis* (London: Home Office Research and Planning Unit)

Beckman, M. (1993) *The 43 Group* (London: Centerprise Publications)

Black to Black (July 1993) *'Racist attacks and harassment'* (London: 1990 Trust) Issue no.1

Bjorgo, T. and Witte, R. (1993) *Racist violence in Europe* (London: The Macmillan Press Limited)

Bottomley, A.K. and Pease, K. (1993) *Crime and Punishment: Interpreting the data* (Milton Keynes: Open University Press)

Bowling, B. (1993) 'Racial harassment and the process of victimisation: conceptual and methodological implications for the local crime survey' in *British Journal of Criminology* Vol.33 No.2 pp. 231-249

Bowling, B. (unpublished) *'Racial harassment in East London'*

Brown, C. (1984) *Black and White Britain* (London: Heinemann Educational Books)

Campaign Against Racism and Fascism (CARF) (1994) 'Deadly Europe' in *CARF* No.18 January/February, pp.4-8

Centre for Multicultural Education (1992) *Sagaland: Youth culture, racism and education* (London: Central Race Equality Unit, London Borough of Greenwich)

Chahal, K. (1992) *Hidden form view: a study of racial harassment in Preston* (Preston: Preston Borough Council)

Commission for Racial Equality (1994) *Annual report: 1993* (London: Commission for Racial Equality)

Commission for Racial Equality (1987) *Living in terror: a report on racial violence and harassment in housing* (London: Commission for Racial Equality)

Committee on Civil Liberties and Internal Affairs (1993) *Report on the resurgence of racism and xenophobia in Europe and the danger of right-wing extremist violence* (Luxembourg: European Parliament)

Committee of Inquiry into the rise of fascism and racism in Europe (1985) *Report of the findings of the Committee of Inquiry* (Luxembourg: European Parliament)

Committee of Inquiry into Racism and Xenophobia (1990) *Report on the findings of the Committee of Inquiry* (Luxembourg: European Parliament)

Cooper, J. and Qureshi, T. (1993) *Through patterns not our own: a study of the regulation of racial violence on the council estates of east London* (London: University of East London)

Department of the Environment (1989) *Tackling racial violence and harassment in local authority housing: a guide to good practice for local authorities* (London: HMSO)

Edwards, S. (1994) 'Domestic violence and sexual assault' in M. Stephens and S. Becker (eds) *Police Force – Police Service: care and control in Britain* (London: Macmillan).

Fekete, L. (1993) 'Inside Racist Europe' in T. Bunyan (ed.) *Statewatching the new Europe* (London: Statewatch) pp.154-172

Fitzgerald, M. and Ellis. T. (1989) 'Racial harassment: the evidence' in C. Kemp (ed.) *Current Issues in Criminological Research: British Criminology Conference 1989* Vol.2 (Bristol: Bristol and Bath Centre for Criminal Justice) pp.51-64

Fitzgerald, M. (1989) 'Racial harassment in Leicester' in *Black Housing* Vol.4 No.3 (London: Federation of black housing organisations) pp.7-12

Ford, G. (1992) *Fascist Europe: The rise of racism and xenophobia* (London: Pluto Press)

Francis, P. and Matthews R. (1993) *Tackling racial attacks* (Leicester: Centre for the Study of Public Order, University of Leicester)

Fryer, P. (1984) *Staying Power: The history of black people in Britain* (London: Pluto Press)

Gilroy, P. (1987) *There ain't no black in the Union Jack* (London: Hutchinson)

Gordon, P. (1989) 'Hidden injuries of racism' in *New Statesman and Society,* 12 May, Vol.2 No.49 pp.24-25

Gordon, P. (1990) *Racial violence and harassment* (London: Runnymede Trust)

Gordon, P. (1992) 'Racist violence and white exclusionism' in *The Runnymede Bulletin*, September, No.258 pp.10-11

Gordon, P. (1993) 'The police and racist violence in Britain' in Bjorgo, T. and Witte, R. (eds) *Racist violence and harassment in Europe* (London: The Macmillan Press Limited)

Hesse, B., Rai, D.K., Bennett, C. and McGilchrist, P. (1992) *Beneath the surface: racial harassment* (Aldershot: Avebury)

Home Affairs Committee (1986) *Racial attacks and harassment* (London: HMSO)

Home Affairs Committee (1989) *Racial attacks and harassment* (London: HMSO)

Home Affairs Committee (1994) *Racial attacks and harassment* (London: HMSO) Volumes 1 and 2

Home Office (1981) *Racial attacks: Report of a Home Office study* (London: Home Office)

Home Office (1989) *The response to racial attacks and harassment: guidance for the statutory agencies* Report of the Inter-Departmental Racial Attacks Group (London: Home Office)

Home Office (1991) *The response to racial attacks: sustaining the momentum* The Second Report of the Inter-Departmental Racial Attacks Group (London: Home Office)

House of Commons (1986) *Racial attacks and harassment* Third report from the Home Affairs Committee, Session 1985-86 (London: HMSO)

Husbands, C. (1994) 'Following the "continental model"?: implications of the recent electoral performance of the British National Party (BNP)' in *New Community* Vol.20 No.4 July, pp.563-579

Institute of Jewish Affairs (1994) *Anti-semitism: world report 1994* (London: Institute of Jewish Affairs)

Jay, E. (1992) *Keep them in Birmingham* (London: Commission for Racial Equality)

Joint Committee Against Racialism (1980) *Racial violence in England* (London: Joint Committee Against Racialism)

Juhnke, A. (1992) 'The hydra-headed monster of Germany' in *New Statesman and Society,* 4 December, Vol.5 No.231 pp.12-13

Kimber, J. and Cooper, L. (1991) *Victim support racial harassment project: final report* (London: Community Research Advisory Centre, Polytechnic of North London)

Kohl, H. (1993) 'Freedom of speech and hate expression: the German experience' in *New Community*, Vol.20 No.1 pp.147-154

Labour Research (1993) 'Racial harassment – the daily hell' in *Labour Research*, July, Vol.82 No.7 pp.7-8

Labour Research (1994) 'Racial attacks: do we need new law?' in *Labour Research*, February, Vol.83 No.2 pp. 7-10

London Research Centre (1993) *London Housing Survey 1992: Harassment in London* (London: London Research Centre)

Love, A-M. and Kirby, K. (1994) *Racial incidents in council housing: the local authority response* (London: HMSO)

Mann, N. (1994) 'The next campaign starts now' in *New Statesman and Society*, 13 May, pp.22-23

Mayhew, P., Elliot, D. and Dowds, L. (1989) *The 1988 British Crime Survey* (London: HMSO)

Mayhew, P., Aye Maung, N. and Mirrlees-Black, C. (1993) *The 1992 British Crime Survey* (London: HMSO)

Miles, R. (1994) 'A rise of racism and fascism in contemporary Europe?: some sceptical reflections on its nature and extent' in *New Community*, Vol.20 No.4, July, pp.547-562

Mirrlees-Black, C. and Aye Maung, N. (1994) *Fear of crime: findings from the 1992 British Crime Survey* (London: Home Office Research and Statistics Department)

Modood, T. (1994) *Racial equality: colour, culture and justice* (London: Institute of Public Policy Research) Commission on Social Justice, Issue Paper No. 5.

Modood, T., Beishon, S. and Virdee, S. (1994) *Changing ethnic identities* (London: Policy Studies Institute)

National Council for Civil Liberties (1993) *Racism: the destruction of civil and political liberties* (London: NCCL)

1990 Trust (1993) *Report on racial attacks and harassment* (London: 1990 Trust)

Norwich and Norfolk Racial Equality Council (1994) *Not in Norfolk: tackling the invisibility of racism* (Norwich: Norwich and Norfolk REC)

Oakley, R. (1992) *Racial violence and harassment in Europe* (Strasbourg: Council of Europe)

Parekh, B. (1994) *Racial violence: a separate offence? A discussion paper* (London: A Charta Mede Associate Company)

Race and Class (1991) *Europe: variations on a theme of racism* Volume 32, January-March, No.3

Ruddock, J. (1993) *Racial attacks – time to act* (London: Labour Party)

Sampson, A. and Phillips, C. (1992) *Multiple victimisation: racial attacks on an east London estate* (London: Home Office Police Department)

Saulsbury, W. and Bowling, B. (1991) *The multi-agency approach in practice: the North Plaistow racial harassment project* (London: Home Office)

Seager, R. and Jeffrey, J. (1994) *Eliminating racial harassment: a guide to housing policies and procedures* (London: Lemos Associates)

Seagrave, J. (1989) *Racially motivated incidents reported to the police* (London: Home Office)

Shaw, C. (1994) *Changing Lives 3* (London: Policy Studies Institute)

Skellington, R. with Morris, P. (1992) *'Race' in Britain today* (London: Sage)

Sivanandan, A. (1993) 'Racism: the road from Germany' in *Race and Class*, Vol.34, January-March, No.3, pp.67-73

Smith, D.J. and Gray, J. (1985) *Police and people in London* (London: Gower Publishing Company Limited)

Stanko, E. (1990) *Everyday violence: how women and men experience sexual and physical danger* (London: Pandora)

Thompson, E.P. (1991) *The making of the English working class* (London: Penguin)

Walsh, D. (1987) *Racial harassment in Glasgow* (Glasgow: Scottish Ethnic Minorities Unit (SEMRU))

Wrench, J., Brar, H. and Martin, P. (1993) *Invisible minorities: racism in new towns and new contexts*, Monographs in ethnic relations, No.6 (Warwick: Centre for Research in Ethnic Relations)

* Additional information was obtained from the CARF magazine, numbers 1-21 (1991-1994).